COOKING
WITH
CHICKEN

WENDY VEALE

A QUANTUM BOOK

This book is produced by
Quantum Publishing Ltd.
6 Blundell Street
London N7 9BH

Copyright © MCMXCVII
Quantum Publishing Ltd

This edition printed 2004

ISBN 1-86160-907-8

QUMCHK-R

Printed in Singapore by
Star Standard Industries Pte Ltd

CONTENTS

INTRODUCTION

CHOOSING THE RIGHT CHICKEN

Chicken rearing and production will determine the flavour and texture of the bird; so will its age. A 'free range' chicken, for example, will have more taste and will need a milder accompaniment than a factory-farmed bird, though it probably won't be as tender. Young birds are ideal for grilling or sautéing – a quick method of sealing in the mild, subtle flavour whilst retaining succulence. Older birds become tough, and require long, slow cooking to tenderize the muscle fibres.

POUSSINS (CORNISH GAME HENS)

These are baby chickens of 4 to 6 weeks old and weighing about 0.5 kg (1 lb). There is not a great deal of flavour in them, and they are best marinaded and then grilled (broiled). A poussin (Cornish game hen) usually serves one person and is available fresh or frozen.

DOUBLE POUSSIN

A chicken weighing around 1 kg (2 to 2¼ lb). Again, they are best grilled (broiled) or spit-roasted.

SPRING CHICKEN

A 12 to 14-week-old chicken averaging 1.1 kg (2½ lb). Roast, spit-roast, grill (broil) or sauté.

BROILERS

A 2 to 4-month-old bird, weighing 1.1 to 1.5 kg (2½ to 3½ lb). One of the most widely sold birds, these are tender but not the most tasty. Grill (broil) or sauté for best results, or roast with a well-flavoured stuffing.

ROASTING CHICKENS

These chickens are 8 to 9 months old and have developed to produce a good flavour. Weighing 1.75 to 2.25 kg (4 to 5 lb), this bird is perfect for roasting and casseroling.

BOILING FOWL

This chicken is usually 12 months old or more and weighs 2.75 to 3.5 kg (6 to 8 lb). It is most suitable for slow casserole cooking or soup and stock making, and cooks well in a pressure cooker. It has a rich flavour and is particularly meaty. Smaller, less plump birds, usually weighing 1.1 to 1.5 kg (2½ to 3½ lb) can also be classified as boiling fowl.

CAPON

This is a cockerel which has been injected with hormone capsules to neuter (caponize) it. It is specially bred to produce a good, meaty roast, and weighs 2.25 to 3.5 kg (5 to 8 lb). Capons are usually sold at Christmas, but have a very small share in the market.

POULARDE

This is a hen which has been neutered to increase its size. As with the capon, a good-sized roaster will be produced, weighing 1.75 kg (4 lb) or over.

CORN-FED CHICKENS

These chickens are specially reared on a diet of maize grains which gives the bird a distinct yellow hue and a good flavour. They are available fresh and are categorized as broilers.

BUYING FRESH CHICKEN

When selecting and buying fresh oven-ready chickens, choose a reputable poulterer, butcher or retailer who has a good, high-quality supplier, a frequent turnover and the time to advise.

Look for a bird with a healthy, pinkish hue, check that it is free from bruising or any other damage, and if it is a roasting bird, the breastbone should be soft and flexible, and the breast plump.

Always check the sell-by date carefully.

STORAGE

FROZEN CHICKENS

When storing a frozen whole chicken, or frozen chicken portions, always follow the instructions on the pack.

Ready-frozen poultry should be transported home as quickly as possible, preferably in an insulated coolbag, and then stored in the home freezer for the recommended time:

RECOMMENDED FREEZER STORAGE PERIODS	
Frozen whole chicken	3 months
Frozen chicken portions	3 months
Cooked chicken	2 months
Giblets	3 months
Boiling Fowl	9 months

FRESH CHICKENS

Fresh chickens, whole or portioned, often carry storage instructions if bought from a large retailer.

If they are already wrapped in packs, the seal should be broken to allow air to circulate, and the chicken to 'breathe'. Otherwise remove wrapping, and giblets if included, and place the chicken on a plate. Cover loosely and put in the lowest (coolest) part of the refrigerator. The chicken will keep for several days.

Ready-cooked chickens should be refrigerated as soon as possible and eaten within 2 to 3 days.

THAWING FROZEN CHICKENS

Frozen chickens must be thoroughly defrosted prior to cooking. If not, and the bird is cooked while still partially frozen, it may not cook all the way through in the recommended time and food poisoning can occur. Therefore, forward planning is important. Ideally a chicken should be thawed in the refrigerator, ensuring that it stays fresh.

The thawing times below are recommended by the British Chicken Information Service given opposite.

Once the bird is defrosted, check to see that there are no ice crystals in the cavity, and that the legs and thighs are pliable. Always ensure that the defrosting bird is on a plate or drip tray and placed at the bottom of the fridge. Otherwise, any uncooked juices from the chicken which drip onto other foods can pass on bacteria and cause food spoilage.

This rule applies to any fresh meat or poultry.

Weight	Thawing at Room Temperature (16°C/65°F)	Thawing in Refrigerator (4°C/39°F)
1 kg (2 lb)	8 hours	28 hours
1.25 kg (3 lb)	9 hours	32 hours
1.75 kg (4 lb)	14 hours	50 hours
3 kg (7 lb)	16 hours	56 hours

METHODS OF COOKING CHICKEN

There are four principal methods of cooking whole and por-tioned chickens, and, as highlighted opposite , the type and age of the chicken will have a great bearing on the most suitable method.

Let's take a look at these principal methods, followed by some alternative and less familiar or obvious cooking methods.

ROASTING

Traditionalists still find great comfort in, and enjoy the ritual of, a roast dinner. It is home cooking at its best and, more often than not, is an occasion shared with a number of family and friends.

Today, roasts are prepared in the oven – the bird or joint is cooked in a current of air by dry (or radiant) heat. An alternative method is the rôtisserie, which is the modern equivalent of true roasting in Medieval Europe. Then, the bird was impaled on a spit and roasted over or in front of an open fire (in fact, true roasting is more like grilling as we know it).

Roasting is only suitable for tender cuts of meat or poultry, as the meat fibres and tissues will shrink and toughen slightly in the initial high temperatures required to seal the outside sur-faces. This 'sealing' ensures that flavoursome juices will be kept in the bird, providing a moister, full-flavoured roast.

Because of its very nature, chicken does not contain a high proportion of fatty tissues and the bird can dry out very quickly during roasting. At one time 'larding' the chicken was common-place. This was done by threading strips of fat (usually bacon) through the flesh. Now, 'barding' is recommended – a much simpler method, overlapping strips of fatty bacon along the breast of the chicken. During cooking, the bacon will 'baste' the chicken and protect it from drying out. The bacon is removed to one side half an hour before the end of cooking to allow the chicken skin to brown and crispen. (And the bacon is not wasted – it's a delicious accompaniment to the bird.)

Mass-produced chickens will benefit from a forcemeat or stuffing. Tucked inside the body cavity, under the breast skin, or both, a stuffing will add both moisture and flavour to the chicken. Meanwhile, below is a guide to the oven temperature and cooking times required for the perfect roast chicken.

Foil will help to retain the bird's natural juices, and also cuts down on the need for basting. However, as the chart shows, additional cooking time is required.

Roasting Bags work well with chicken. Not only do they help keep the oven clean, but they also self-baste and brown the chicken. They are available in a variety of sizes. It is important to pierce the bag, or cut away a corner, to allow the steam to escape. This not only ensures that the chicken will brown and crispen, but also prevents the bag from exploding!

Basting. As well as barding the chicken breasts with fatty bacon, brushing the chicken with a little oil or melted butter before roasting helps to protect the flesh and crispen the skin. Baste the chicken regularly – every 15 to 20 minutes or so – to keep it moist.

IS THE CHICKEN COOKED?

Insert a thin skewer into the thickest part of the thigh. If the juices run out clear, then the bird is cooked. Alternatively, tip the chicken up and examine the juices escaping from the body cavity. Again, the should be clear.

The leg is also a good indicator: the meat tends to shrink from the end of the drumstick and the leg, when tugged gently away from the body, will 'give'.

RELAXING

Once any joint or whole bird is cooked, it needs some 'standing time' on a hot dish in a warm place. This allows for all the juices which, during cooking, have drawn up to the surface of the chicken to redistribute back into the flesh. Allow 10 to 15 minutes for this. It is well worthwhile, producing a better, more succulent texture and making carving easier.

2 POT ROASTING, BRAISING OR CASSEROLING

Pot Roasting is the equivalent of the French method of braising.

Chicken Weight	Cooking Time	Oven Temp	Stuffed Bird	Foil Wrapped Bird
1.5 kg and under (3½ lb)	20 mins per 500 g/lb + 20 mins extra	190°C/375°F/Gas 5	Add 20–25 mins extra to the overall time	Add 15 mins extra to the overall time. Pull back the foil for last 20 mins. cooking time to allow chicken to brown.
1.75 kg–2.75 kg (4–6 lb)	25 mins per 500 g/lb + 25 mins extra	170°C/325°F/Gas 3	Add 20–25 mins extra to the overall time	Add 15 mins extra to the overall time. Pull back the foil for last 20 mins. cooking time to allow chicken to brown.

It is a combination of a type of stew and roast. Whereas a traditional roast can take up time and attention, a pot roast, or braise, allows you to use older, tougher joints and birds which require longer, slower methods of cooking, and leave you free to attend to other things. A French braising pan or a cast-iron casserole which can be used both over direct heat and in the oven is ideal. These need a tight-fitting lid, otherwise flavouring juices will evaporate and escape.

The principle of pot roasting or braising is to first seal the chicken over a direct heat and then add some herbs, vegetables and just enough stock or wine to cover the vegetables. The liquid will baste and keep the chicken moist, and can then be used in an accompanying sauce. Once the lid is fitted on and the pot roast is transferred to a slow oven (170°C/325°F/Gas 3), the chicken will cook in a moist, steamy atmosphere. The lid may be removed, and the heat increased for a short time towards the end of the cooking period to brown and roast the surface of the chicken.

Cooking time is about 25 per cent longer than roasting, but it is well worth it, as the bird will be tender and very succulent.

Casseroling is a long, slow method of cooking chicken and meats in the oven (not to be confused with stewing which takes place on top of the cooker). Vegetables, herbs and stock or wine are added to the sealed whole chicken, or portions, and it is then given just enough heat to simmer the liquid gently for as long as is required to tenderize the tougher older bird. A well-fitting lid, again, is important to retain the juices.

3 SAUTÉING, SHALLOW & DEEP FAT FRYING

Fried foods have, over the past few years, become taboo. Associations with saturated fats, cholesterol and heart problems have steered the majority of us away to more healthy methods of cooking.

However, there are some recipes which cannot, and indeed, should not avoid this integral method of cooking.

Sautéing is often required to seal and brown chicken portions before transferring them to a casserole dish. Sautéing is an excellent method of cooking chicken pieces; it keeps them tender and succulent, is an easy and quick method of cooking, and is the healthiest way of savouring 'fried' foods.

'Sauté' derives from the French verb 'sauter' – to jump. Although the flick of the wrist will not be required to continually toss the chicken (so making it jump), the portions will need to be turned frequently to maintain a golden brown colour and ensure even cooking. With the range of polyunsaturated fats now available, and good non-stick frying pans on the market, sautéed chicken can be included in a healthy eating plan.

The French may sauté, but the Chinese stir-fry in a wok!

Shallow Frying requires the chicken portion, first coated in seasoned flour or eggs and breadcrumbs, to be half submerged in 1.25 cm (½ in) hot oil or fat. The result is a crispy outer 'shell' concealing a moist and succulent chicken portion. The chicken will require turning half way through cooking. Take care not to over-crowd the pan, as this can not only cause the food to overlap and 'steam', but it also lowers the temperature causing the food to absorb unnecessary oil. Choose a polyunsaturated oil such as sunflower or corn oil to shallow fry in.

Deep Fat Frying. Deep fried chicken drumsticks, sizzling in golden oil, can be enough to tempt even the strictest of healthy food followers. A light, crisp batter, concealing a juicy chicken wing or perhaps the breadcrumbed Russian version concealing butter, garlicky juices of Chicken Kiev, are enough to cause the most dedicated and calorie-conscious amongst us to waiver. Once in a while we can cope with such indulgences – but it is best not to make a habit of it!

Deep-fried foods are fattening and often indigestible. The latter is due to the oil being too cool, either from overloading the pan with too much food, or underheating the oil. The protective batter or breadcrumb coating on the food will not instantly seal and, instead, absorbs the oil. The food becomes greasy and soggy, rather than crisp and appetising. On the other hand, if the oil is too hot, the 'shell' will brown too quickly and possibly burn on the outside before cooking the contents.

Careful cooking is required at a temperature of between 180 and 190°C (350–375°F), and don't forget the polyunsaturated oil. At least that will help ease the conscience a little.

4 GRILLING (BROILING) & BARBECUING

Grilling (broiling) is a very similar cooking method to roasting. The obvious difference, however, is that instead of surrounding the chicken with a dry, intense heat in an oven cavity, grilling radiates heat from one direction – above, or as in the case of a barbecue, below.

Grilling (broiling) is a delicious method of cooking the most tender, small chickens, poussins (Cornish game hens) and portions. It is a quick method, but requires constant attention, turning the chicken, sealing it on all sides and occasionally basting it.

Because the younger chicken may lack maturity, a marinade is an excellent way of adding flavour before cooking.
It can also be brushed on the bird as it grills, to prevent it from drying out.

Barbecuing. When cooking on a barbecue, sprigs of fresh herbs sprinkled on the coals will emit appetizing smells.

Having provided a brief resumé of the four main methods of cooking chicken, here are other suitable, although less used, methods of cooking.

1 THE CHICKEN BRICK

This is a very healthy and under-estimated method of cooking a whole roasting chicken. The chicken is placed in a clay chicken brick (which has previously been soaked in water for 25 minutes), and then simply placed in a preheated oven and cooked for the usual recommended times, but at a high temperature. Because the chicken will cook in its own juices, no added fats or basting is required; the chicken retains its own flavour and nutrients.

2 THE MICROWAVE OVEN

Chickens can be successfully defrosted and cooked in the microwave oven, and once the manufacturer's instructions have been carefully read, and the method mastered, the results are moist and tender. However, as with all alternative methods of cooking, a little practice will make perfect. The following chart shows the different cooking times determined by the power of the microwave oven.

Chicken	Quantity	Cooking Times		
		400W	500–600W	650–700W
Whole bird. Place breast side down in pierced roasting bag, using rack to keep meat clear of juices. Allow to stand for 15–20 minutes, wrapped in foil.	500 g (1 lb)	12	8	6
	1 kg (2 lb)	20	14	10
	1.5 kg (3 lb)	28	20	15
	1.75 kg (4 lb)	38	26	21
	2.25 kg (5 lb)	50	33	26
	2.7 kg (6 lb)	62	40	32
Chicken portion with bone*	2 portions	12	8	6
	4 portions	17	13	9
Chicken portion without bone (eg breast)**	2 portions	8	5	4
	4 portions	12	8	6

* Arrange in single layer with thinner end towards centre.
**Brush with oil or melted butter, turning over once during cooking.

3 PRESSURE COOKING
This is a quick and economical method of cooking chicken, but as with the microwave oven, models vary and instructions must be followed carefully.

4 STEAMING
Steaming is a quick, natural and healthy way of cooking and an excellent method of retaining nutrients and flavour. This moist method of cooking is ideal for chicken which does have a tendency to dry out easily. A 250 g (8 oz) breast will require 20 to 25 minutes, and a 250 g (8 oz) leg, 30 to 35 minutes.

5 ELECTRIC SLOW COOKING
Slow cookers are useful for the person with a hectic lifestyle. It allows long, slow cooking completely unattended. It is the same cooking method, in principle, as braising and casseroling, but sits on the worktop and is plugged in to an electrical power point. The long period of cooking in a moist atmosphere will tenderize the toughest of birds. A 1.5 kg (3½ lb) whole chicken will take 4 hours on the high setting to cook, but will sit quite happily for another hour without spoiling. Always refer to the manufacturer's instruction book before using.

6 POACHING
Poaching is carried out in 'shivering' as opposed to 'simmering' water. Because of the low cooking temperature, true poaching is only applicable to fish and eggs.

However, for poultry, the water or stock is kept just under the boil, at a steady simmer. The results, though simple, are delicious. The chicken is moist and tender, any accompanying garden vegetables are full of flavour, and the resulting broth can be made into a wholesome soup or stock.

Henry IV of France declared 'I want there to be no peasant in my kingdom so poor that he cannot have a chicken in his pot every Sunday' – hence the famous 'poulet au pot'.

PORTIONING, CARVING & JOINTING

PORTIONING
Depending on whether you are buying a chicken whole or already conveniently portioned, there can still be room for doubt over the quantity of meat to allow per person.

Chicken portions – part-boned or boneless breasts, legs, quarters, wings, thighs and drumsticks are one of the easiest options.

The size and number of portions to allow depends very much on the recipe involved, and your own appetite. And, of course, the size of the original chicken also has a great bearing. Here is an approximate guide:

Portion per person	Cooked plainly	Cooked in sauce or with other ingredients
Part-boned breast	175–250 g (6–8 oz)	125–175 g (4–6 oz)
Boneless breast	175 g (6 oz)	125 g (4 oz)–150 g (5 oz)
Chicken quarter	300–375 g (10–12 oz)	300 g (10 oz)
Chicken leg	250–300 g (8–10 oz)	200–250 g 7–8 oz)
Chicken thighs	3	2
Chicken wings	4–6	2–4
Chicken drumsticks	3	2
Cold cooked chicken meat	175 g (6 oz)	125 g (4 oz)

Allowances have been made for general wastage – skin, bones, etc.

For chickens to be cooked whole, there is a standard rule of thumb which works well and provides a certain amount of leeway.

For each person, allow 375 to 500 g (¾ to 1 lb). So, for example, a 1.1 to 1.25 kg (2½ to 3 lb) chicken will serve 2 to 3 people, a 1.75 to 2.25 kg (4 to 5 lb) chicken will serve 4 to 5 people, and so on.

CARVING A CHICKEN
Always allow the cooked chicken to 'stand' for 15 minutes before carving. Not only is the bird more succulent, but the flesh and juices have 'relaxed' and make carving easier.

If you don't have your own 'trencher' in the household do make sure you have a sturdy non-slip carving plate or board and a long sharp carving knife and fork. Carving poultry is simple if you follow these basic guidelines:

(i) Press the thigh down and away from the chicken body to reveal the leg joint. Secure the chicken with the fork and insert the knife between the body and leg to remove the leg. Separate the drumstick from the thigh to produce two leg portions (unless the bird is very small).

(ii) To remove the wing, take a line from the top of the wishbone right down through the joint, to include a reasonable portion of breast meat.

(iii) Thinly slice the remaining breast.

(iv) Repeat with the other side of the bird. Don't forget to remove the 'oysters', two tiny meaty delicacies positioned in hollows on each side of the back.

JOINTING A CHICKEN

A little awesome at first, but certainly nothing to worry about. Nature provided the chicken with obvious incision lines – all you need is a sharp boning knife and a pair of poultry shears (good kitchen scissors or secateurs will do).

You may find a fresh chicken much easier to handle than a thawed 'frozen' chicken which may be more slippery.

This method provides 8 small portions.

(i) To remove the legs: stretch the leg outward as far as you can and cut through the natural line dividing the leg from the breast. Pull the thigh bone back at the bottom to reveal the joint. Cut through. Repeat with the other leg.

(ii) Turn the leg over, find the thin white line at the centre of the joint and cut through it. Repeat with the remaining leg. Now you have 4 portions.

(iii) To remove each breast: carefully cut down one side of the breastbone, scraping with the knife to remove the flesh from the bone, while carefully lifting the flesh away, taking the wing with it. Repeat on the other side.

(iv) Lay the breasts on a chopping board and cut each in half diagonally, so that the wing has a section of breast with it.

You now have 8 portions.

There are other methods of jointing a chicken, to produce anything from 4 to 10 portions.

If there are any bones remaining, use them to make stock.

Once this skill is acquired, it does not take long to joint a bird. However, if you are hesitant or in doubt, your friendly butcher should oblige.

NOTES ON THE RECIPES

Ingredients are given in American, metric and imperial measures. Use only one set of quantities, for any one recipe.

All spoon measurements are level unless specified.

Half a teaspoonful (½ tsp) = 2.5 ml
One teaspoonful (1 tsp) = 5 ml
One tablespoonful (1 tbsp) = 15 ml

WEIGHTS AND MEASURES

Metric	American/Imperial
15 g	½ oz
25 g	1 oz
125 g	4 oz
250 g	8 oz
375 g	12 oz
500 g	1 lb
750 g	1½ lb
1 kg	2 lb
1.25 kg	3 lb
1.75 kg	4 lb

VOLUME (liquid)

American	Metric	Imperial
¼ cup	60 ml	4 tbsp
	100 ml	3 fl oz
½ cup	125 ml	4 fl oz
	150 ml	5 fl oz/¼ pt
	200 ml	7 fl oz
1¼ cup	300 ml	10 fl oz/½ pt
1½ cup	375 ml	12 fl oz
2½ cup	600 ml	20 fl oz/1 pt
	750 ml	1¼ pt
	900 ml	1½ pt
	1.2 l	2 pt
	1.75 l	3 pt

OVEN TEMPERATURES

Ovens should be preheated to the temperature specified.

130 °C	250 °F	Gas ½
140 °C	275 °F	Gas 1
150 °C	300 °F	Gas 2
160 °C	325 °F	Gas 3
180 °C	350 °F	Gas 4
190 °C	375 °F	Gas 5
200 °C	400 °F	Gas 6
220 °C	425 °F	Gas 7

Eggs are standard size 3, ie medium, unless otherwise stated.

When fresh herbs are unavailable, use dried herbs but halve the quantity, unless otherwise indicated.

BASIC RECIPES

RAYMOND BLANC'S BROWN CHICKEN STOCK BROTH

A dark, brown chicken stock is used for the stronger flavoured, richer sauces and casseroles. Although this recipe may seem a great deal of effort for so small a quantity of juices, it is well worth it.

- ☐ In a large roasting pan, heat the vegetable oil until smoking, then brown the chicken wings or carcasses for 8 to 10 minutes, stirring occasionally with a wooden spoon.
- ☐ In a small bowl mix the peppercorns, onion, garlic, thyme and bayleaf, then add to the chicken and cook for a further 5 minutes. Transfer to the oven and cook for 20 minutes or until a rich brown.
- ☐ Meanwhile brush the tomatoes with a little vegetable oil and cook them in the oven for 10 minutes until brown. Add to the chicken wings or carcass. Transfer the roasting pan to the hob.
- ☐ Deglaze the roasting pan with 1 cup/200 ml/7 fl oz of the water, scraping up all the caramelized juices from the bottom of the pan. Add the remaining water, bring to the boil, and return to the hot oven for 20 minutes.
- ☐ Strain the juices into a small saucepan, bring to the boil, skim and reduce to about 2¼ cups/500 ml/18 fl oz tasty clear brown stock. Cool, then refrigerate.
- ☐ Remove any fat which has settled on the surface, seal with cling film (plastic wrap) and store until needed.

This stock can be made in advance and kept in the fridge for 1 week or in the freezer for 3 weeks.

VARIATIONS

CHICKEN DEMI-GLACE
Reduce the juices by half.

CHICKEN GLAZE
Reduce the juices to ⅓ cup/90 ml/6 tbsp to obtain a concentrated essence.

MAKES APPROX 2 ¼ CUPS/ 500 ML/18 FL OZ

1.5 kg/3½ lb chicken wings or carcasses
⅓ cup/90 ml/6 tbsp vegetable oil
6 black peppercorns, crushed
1 medium onion, finely chopped
1 clove garlic, crushed (minced)
1 sprig thyme
½ bayleaf
4 medium tomatoes, halved
3¾ cups/900 ml/1½ pint water

Oven temperature: 230 °C/450 °F/Gas 8

15 ml/1 tbsp vegetable oil
1 onion, finely chopped
2 small Cox's Orange Pippin apples
(or sweet dessert apples)
10 ml/2 teaspoons fresh rosemary, chopped
2 cups/125 g/4 oz fresh white breadcrumbs
salt and freshly ground black pepper
1 egg yolk, beaten

STUFFINGS

Stuffings or forcemeats date back to the Middle Ages and their main purpose is to help keep the poultry flesh moist, to counteract any greasiness, and the herbs which are often included, were thought to aid digestion and stimulate the appetite.

Here are 4 different stuffings which are all suitable for poultry and provide a good basis for you to experiment and slightly amend the ingredients and flavourings. Each recipe yields sufficient for a 1.75 kg/4 lb chicken.

TO STUFF THE BREAST

☐ Starting at the neck end gently loosen the skin away from the breast to form a pocket.

☐ Using your fingers, work in some stuffing, evenly smoothing it down to form a rounded mound. Do not put too much stuffing in, as, during cooking, it will swell slightly and may break the skin.

☐ Fold the loose neck flap of skin back under the bird and secure with a cocktail stick or small skewer.

Simply spoon any remaining mixture into the bird's cavity or roll the stuffing into small balls and place in the roasting tin alongside the bird 30 minutes before the end of cooking.

NOTE

Remember to adjust the roasting times for stuffed birds (see page 7).

ROSEMARY & APPLE STUFFING

Heat the oil in a pan and sauté the onion until softened. Meanwhile, peel, core and finely chop the apples. Remove pan from heat and combine all the ingredients together.

1 cup/175 g/6 oz coarse oatmeal
¼ cup/50 g/2 oz butter, melted
1 large onion, finely chopped
2 pinches grated nutmeg
15 ml/1 tbsp mixed dried herbs
45 ml/3 tbsp whisky or stock (broth)
salt and freshly ground black pepper

OATMEAL STUFFING (SKIRLIE)

Combine all the ingredients together, adding a little extra liquid if necessary to make a moist mixture.

2 cups/125 g/4 oz fresh white breadcrumbs
½ stick celery, finely chopped
grated rind 1 small lemon
45 ml/3 tbsp freshly chopped parsley
10 ml/2 tsp freshly chopped thyme
salt and ground black pepper, to taste
2 tbsp/25 g/1 oz butter, melted
1 egg yolk, beaten

LEMON, PARSLEY & THYME STUFFING

Combine all the ingredients together in a bowl. Mix thoroughly.

2 tbsp/25 g/1 oz butter
1 medium onion, finely chopped
½ cup/125 g/4 oz dried apricots (non-soak variety)
¼ cup/50 g/2 oz blanched almonds, coarsely chopped
30 ml/2 tbsp chopped fresh chives, sage and parsley
1 cup/125 g/4 oz brown rice, cooked
1 egg yolk, beaten
salt and freshly ground black pepper, to taste

FRUIT & NUTTY RICE SALAD

Melt the butter in a pan and cook the onion until softened. Stir in the remaining ingredients, mixing thoroughly.

BREAD SAUCE

Bread sauce dates back to Medieval times and has remained a traditional accompaniment to roast chicken and turkey ever since. The purpose of the breadcrumbs was originally to thicken a sauce in the absence of a stove for simmering and reducing.

☐ Gently warm the milk in a saucepan, to just under boiling point. Remove.

☐ Stick the cloves into the onion, and add to the milk together with the peppercorns, bayleaf and mace. Leave the milk to stand for 30 minutes to allow the flavours to infuse.

☐ Add the breadcrumbs, butter and seasoning and return to a very gentle heat for 10 minutes. Remove the onion, cloves, peppercorns, bayleaf and mace. Check seasoning. Stir in the cream (optional).

☐ Serve immediately in a sauce boat to accompany the roast chicken.

NOTE
Bread sauce is not suitable for freezing.

MARINADES FOR BARBECUED CHICKEN

A marinade is, very often, a highly seasoned or flavoured liquid – perhaps with the addition of spices, herbs or citrus fruits. Marinating flavours food such as fish, meat, game and poultry and even vegetables. It can tenderize tougher cuts, give moisture to dry meats and preserves the food for a day or two longer than normal. The marinade can also act as a barbecue sauce, to baste the grilled or roast meats.

The first two liquid marinades are excellent for chicken. Simply mix the ingredients together. Quantities are enough for a 1.75 kg/3½ lb chicken or equivalent parts.

☐ Lay the chicken joints or pieces in a shallow dish. Pour over the marinade.

☐ Turn the chicken, to coat thoroughly.

☐ Cover with cling film (plastic wrap) and leave at room temperature for 2 to 3 hours, or chill for 8 hours, preferably overnight.

☐ Drain the chicken and cook accordingly. Baste the chicken with the remaining marinade, turning the chicken frequently.

If you are wanting to roast or grill a whole or jointed chicken with a difference, the simple and speedy infusion of flavours given by a dry marinade is perfect. Because of the high salt content, the marinade should only be on the chicken for 1 hour.

☐ Crush the garlic cloves with the flat blade of a heavy chopping knife, or alternatively, use a pestle and mortar.

☐ Add the other ingredients and work them together until they are reduced to a paste.

☐ Spread the surface of the chicken with the marinade. Cover and leave to stand for 1 hour.

☐ Scrape off and discard the marinade before cooking the chicken.

TO MAKE 1¼ CUP/300 ML/ ½ PINT

1¼ cups/300 ml/½ pt milk
1 medium onion, peeled
4 cloves
6 black peppercorns
1 bayleaf
1 small piece mace
1 cup/50 g/2 oz fresh white breadcrumbs
2 tbsp/25 g/1 oz butter
salt and white pepper
15 ml/1 tbsp single (light) cream (optional)

WHITE WINE MARINADE

¼ cup/60 ml/4 tbsp white wine
30 ml/2 tbsp olive oil
30 ml/2 tbsp lemon juice
5 ml/1 tsp mustard powder
1 clove garlic, finely chopped
4 black peppercorns
1 bayleaf
1 sprig tarragon (optional)
1 strip lemon peel

YOGURT MARINADE

⅔ cup/150 ml/¼ pt natural yogurt
30 ml/2 tbsp tomato ketchup
30 ml/2 tbsp olive oil
15 ml/1 tbsp Worcestershire sauce
10 ml/2 tsp clear honey
5 ml/1 tsp mustard powder
dash Tabasco
1 shallot, finely chopped
2 cloves garlic, finely chopped

DRY CHICKEN MARINADE

4 cloves garlic
5 ml/1 tsp dried thyme
2.5 ml/½ tsp ground bayleaves
8 black peppercorns, crushed
30 ml/2 tbsp coarse salt
15 ml/1 tbsp lemon juice

CHICKEN AND WALNUT TERRINE

The French word 'terrine' originally meant an earthenware dish, but nowadays refers to its contents. This needs to be made a day or two in advance to develop the flavours, and should be served cold, sliced, with a salad garnish and wholemeal bread.

☐ Sauté half the chicken liver in the oil until just browned. Remove and cut into thin strips. Cut the chicken breast into thin strips and put in a bowl with the cooked livers, the sherry, brandy and peppercorns. Cover and leave to marinade for 2 hours.

☐ Put the remaining chicken livers and the pork in a food processor and blend together with the egg, garlic and salt, until the mixture is smooth.

☐ Place one third of this mixture in a lightly greased 5 cup/1.2 1/2 pt terrine or loaf tin (pan), and cover with half the chicken strips and half the walnuts.

☐ Cover with another third of the pork mixture, and then the rest of the chicken strips and walnuts. Spread the remaining pork mixture over the top. Cover with foil.

☐ Place on a baking tray (cookie sheet), and bake for 1 hour. Cool, top off any liquid and then chill, preferably overnight.

☐ Serve in slices, garnished with an assortment of salad leaves and, if you like, spring onion (scallion) flowers.

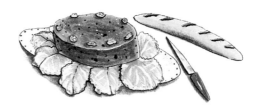

Chicken Livers in Jackets

CHICKEN LIVERS IN JACKETS

Inexpensive to make and quick to produce, these little rolls of crisp bacon encasing chicken livers will soon vanish with the cocktails! The fruits listed below are just a suggestion of what to serve with the chicken livers, but almost any fruit works well.

☐ Drain the chicken livers, if necessary, and remove any threads. Cut each into pieces the size of a small walnut.

☐ Using the back of a heavy knife, stretch the bacon rashers lengthways on a large chopping board. Cut each rasher into 2 to 3 equal lengths, each long enough to wrap around a piece of chicken liver.

☐ Roll the bacon lengths around the chicken livers. Push a thin bamboo skewer (pre-soaked for ½ hour to prevent burning) through the centre of each roll. Lay on a rack in a grill pan or small roasting tin. Cook for 10 to 15 minutes in the oven, or under a preheated grill (broiler), until sizzling and crisp. Remove skewers.

☐ Meanwhile, prepare the fruit. Cut the banana into thick slices, halve the kiwi fruit lengthwise and cut into thick slices.

☐ Thread each bacon roll and a piece of fruit onto cocktail sticks and serve immediately.

COCK-A-LEEKIE SOUP

Scotland is thought to be the home of this substantial soup – although the Welsh may agree to differ! The bird that ended up in the stock pot may originally have been the loser of a cock-fight. Long simmering is required but the result is well worth waiting for.

☐ Place the chicken in a large, heavy-based saucepan. Add the onion, carrots, celery, bayleaf, bouquet garni, peppercorns and salt. Cover with the water.
☐ Bring the pan very gently to the boil, skim, and then simmer for about 2 hours or until the chicken is tender. Strain off the stock, discarding the cooked vegetables, and leave to cool, then chill in the refrigerator until the fat hardens and can be easily removed. Alternatively, clean off all the grease from the hot stock with absorbent kitchen paper (paper towel). Remove the skin from the chicken and cut the flesh into thin strips.
☐ Melt the butter in a large pan, add the leeks and spring onions (scallions) and cook over a low heat for 10 minutes. Add the rice and allspice and cook for a further 5 minutes. Pour on the skimmed stock, bring to the boil and simmer for 15 minutes. Add the chicken and simmer for a further 10 minutes, season to taste, mix in the parsley and serve.

SERVES 4 TO 6

I small boiling or roasting chicken
(approx. 1.1–1.5 kg/2½–3½ lb)
1 onion, quartered
2 carrots, chopped
1 stick celery, chopped
1 bayleaf
1 bouquet garni
6 peppercorns
5 ml/1 tsp salt
7½ cups/1.75 l/3 pt water
2 tbsp/25 g/1 oz butter
4 leeks, trimmed and thinly sliced
2 spring onions (scallions), trimmed and thinly sliced
¼ cup/25 g/1 oz long grain rice
pinch allspice
15 ml/1 tbsp chopped parsley

ORIENTAL CHICKEN NOODLE SOUP

Soup is included in almost every meal in Thailand and China and, contrary to Western custom, the soup is eaten together with other dishes, or even at the end of the meal. What is common worldwide, though, is that the basis of a good soup is the stock.

☐ Cut the chicken into thin strips. Soak the mushrooms in warm water for 15 minutes. Drain well, squeezing out excess moisture. Cut away and discard the stems and shred the caps.
☐ Bring the chicken stock to a steady simmer. Add the chicken, mushrooms, noodles, sugar, soy sauce, sherry or rice wine and pepper to taste. Simmer for 15 minutes or until the chicken and noodles are tender.
☐ Stir in the spring onions, red chilli (chili) flakes, chopped coriander (cilantro) and sesame oil
☐ Pour into individual bowls and serve immediately.

SERVES 4 TO 6

250 g/8 oz boneless chicken meat (breast or thigh)
4 dried Chinese mushrooms
4½ cups/1.2 l/2 pt chicken stock (broth)
(see page 12)
2 bundles rice vermicelli noodles (approx. 150 g/5 oz)
10 ml/2 tsp sugar
30 ml/2 tsp dark soy sauce
45 ml/3 tbsp dry sherry or rice wine
white pepper
4 spring onions (scallions), cut diagonally into
2 cm/1 in strips
15 ml/1 tbsp dried red chilli (chili) flakes
15 ml/1 tbsp fresh coriander (cilantro), chopped
10 ml/2 tsp sesame oil

500 g/1 lb chicken livers
⅓ cup/90 ml/6 tbsp ruby port
2 cloves garlic, crushed (minced)
10 ml/2 tsp fresh thyme, chopped
2.5 ml/½ tsp grated nutmeg
2 tbsp/25 g/1 oz butter
¼ cup/60 ml/4 tbsp fromage frais or double (heavy)
cream
salt and freshly ground black pepper
5 ml/1 tsp powdered gelatine (gelatin)
⅔ cup/150 ml/¼ pt chicken stock (broth)

GARNISH
bay leaves
peppercorns
stuffed olives

Oven temperature: 180 °C/350 °F/Gas 4

CHICKEN LIVER PÂTÉ

A very good pâté – quick to make and best served with melba toast or french bread. Try it too, as a cânapé, spooned into small mushroom caps or hollowed out cherry tomatoes.

☐ Trim and wash the livers, and cut in half. Put them in a bowl with the port, garlic, thyme and nutmeg. Mix the ingredients well, cover and marinade for 2 hours. Drain the livers, reserving the juices.

☐ Melt the butter in a frying pan, add the drained livers, and sauté for a few minutes or until the livers change colour.

☐ Add the reserved juices and simmer, uncovered, for a further minute. Cool slightly. Season to taste.

☐ Blend or process the liver mixture together with the fromage frais or cream until smooth. Pour into a small serving dish (or 4 individual ramekin dishes). Cover and place in a roasting tin half filled with water. Cook for 40 minutes.

☐ Sprinkle the gelatine (gelatin) into the hot chicken stock. Dissolve over a pan of hot water (or microwave on HIGH at 600W for 30 seconds). Cool to room temperature, or until just syrupy.

☐ Arrange the bayleaves, peppercorns and stuffed olive slices on top of the pâté. Carefully spoon a thin layer of the gelatine (gelatin) mixture over. Chill until set.

NOTE
The made up pâté will freeze for up to 2 months, after cooking, but before the gelatine (gelatin) is applied.

CHICKEN AND SPINACH TERRINE

A perfect start to a dinner party, or as a main course for a summer lunch. Serve on its own, or with new potatoes and a fresh crisp green salad.

- ☐ For the spinach mixture, mix the spinach with nutmeg, salt and pepper to taste. Blend in the fromage frais and egg yolks.
- ☐ Dissolve the gelatine (gelatin) in 30 ml/2 tbsp water (place in a basin over a pan of simmering water). Allow to cool slightly before stirring into the spinach mixture.
- ☐ For the chicken mixture, heat the oil and stir-fry the minced chicken for 4 to 5 minutes. Do not allow it to brown.
- ☐ Add the garlic, green peppercorns, salt and pepper to taste, and the Vermouth. Bubble briskly for 1 minute.
- ☐ Blend the chicken in a liquidizer or food processor until smooth. Stir the pistachio nuts and fromage frais into the chicken mixture.
- ☐ Dissolve the gelatine (gelatin) in 45 ml/3 tbsp water (as above) and add to the chicken mixture; blend well.
- ☐ Put half the chicken mixture into a lightly oiled and lined 1 kg/2 lb loaf tin (pan), cover carefully with the spinach mixture, and spread the remaining chicken mixture over the top. Chill until the terrine is firm enough to slice.
- ☐ Meanwhile, make the sauce. Put the yogurt, watercress and garlic into a liquidizer or food processor and blend until smooth. Stir in the white wine and season to taste.
- ☐ Carefully unmould (unmold) the set terrine and cut into slices. Place a slice on each serving plate, and spoon a pool of sauce around the terrine. Garnish with a few extra green peppercorns or a sprig of fresh dill.

SERVES 8 TO 10

SPINACH MIXTURE
500 g/1 lb cooked spinach, well drained and chopped
freshly grated nutmeg
salt and freshly ground black pepper
⅔ cup/150 ml/¼ pt fromage frais (low fat)
2 egg yolks
10 ml/2 tsp powdered gelatine (gelatin)

CHICKEN MIXTURE
15 ml/1 tbsp vegetable oil
700 g/1 ½ lb boneless chicken, minced
1 clove garlic, crushed (minced)
5 ml/1 tsp green peppercorns
salt and freshly ground black pepper
¼ cup/60 ml/4 tbsp dry Vermouth
25 g/1 oz pistachio nuts
¾ cup/175 ml/6 fl oz fromage frais (low fat)
15 ml/3 tsp powdered gelatine (gelatin)

SAUCE
scant cup/200 ml/⅓ pt thick natural yogurt (preferably low fat)
1 bunch watercress, washed and trimmed
1 whole clove garlic, peeled
¼ cup/60 ml/4 tbsp dry white wine
salt and freshly ground black pepper

GARNISH
a few green peppercorns or a sprig of dill

AVOCADO AND CHICKEN SALAD

This is a quick, yet delicious, way of using up any left-over cooked chicken – a perfect summer lunch. Try ringing the changes with mango instead of avocado.

☐ Split the avocado in half, remove the stone (pit) and skin and cut into neat slices. Brush with the lemon juice to prevent discoloration.

☐ Slice each tomato and arrange alternately with the avocado around the outer edge of a flat serving plate, as shown.

☐ Mix the chicken with the spring onions, parsley and nuts. Whisk together the Garlic Vinaigrette ingredients. There should be enough to coat the chicken well.

☐ Pile the mixture in the centre of the plate. Brush any remaining dressing over the avocado and tomato slices. Garnish with a sprinkling of parsley.

Avocado and Chicken Salad

Hot Chicken and Spinach Salad

HOT CHICKEN AND SPINACH SALAD

☐ Rinse and lightly shake the spinach leaves. Tear into pieces and place in a bowl or on individual serving plates. Sprinkle on the spring onions (scallions), hazelnuts and courgettes (zucchini).

☐ Cut the chicken into thin strips. Heat two thirds of the oil in a large, shallow pan and briskly stir-fry the chicken with the onion and garlic until just tender.

☐ Stir in the remaining olive oil, wine vinegar, salt and pepper and tarragon. Allow to cook for a further minutes. Spoon the hot chicken and dressing over the salad ingredients.

☐ Sprinkle with the diced sweet red (bell) pepper and serve immediately.

CHICKEN WITH SEAFOOD SAUCE

An unusual combination of fowl and fish which tastes exceptionally good. Serve with a crisp green salad and new potatoes.

- ☐ Place the chicken in a large pan with the pared lemon rind, sliced onion, bayleaf and white wine. Add sufficient water to come halfway up the chicken.
- ☐ Chop 4 of the anchovy fillets and add them and the reserved prawn (shrimp) shells to the pan, season, cover and bring to the boil, then simmer for about 1½ hours or until the chicken is tender.
- ☐ Meanwhile, make the sauce. Blend together the mayonnaise, lemon juice, 1 tablespoonful of the capers and the drained tuna fish. When smooth, season with salt and pepper to taste.
- ☐ Remove the cooked chicken to a carving dish. Add sufficient of the strained cooking liquid to the tuna fish sauce to give a smooth, coating consistency.
- ☐ Carve the cooked chicken while still warm and arrange on a flat platter. Spoon the prepared sauce over the top. Chill. Garnish the chicken with the peeled prawns (shrimp), remaining anchovy fillets, capers and fresh basil.

SERVES 4

1 oven-ready chicken (about 1.5 kg/3½ lbs)
thinly pared rind of 1 lemon
1 small onion, thinly sliced
1 bayleaf
1¼ cups/300 ml/½ pt dry white wine
10 anchovy fillets
24 prawns (shrimp), peeled and shells reserved
salt and freshly ground black pepper
1¼ cups/300 ml/½ pt low calorie mayonnaise
juice of ½ lemon
30 ml/2 tbsp capers
200 g/7 oz can tuna fish in brine
fresh basil sprigs to garnish

3 ripe peaches
1 ¼ cups/300 ml/½ pt dry white wine
2 strips lemon peel
15 ml/1 tbsp fresh tarragon, chopped
(or 2.5 ml/½ tsp dried)
salt and freshly ground black pepper
4 chicken breasts (approx. 150 g/5 oz each)
chicken stock (broth)
⅔ cup/150 ml/¼ pt fromage frais (preferably low fat)

GARNISH
Slices of skinned fresh peach (optional)
fresh tarragon sprigs

CHICKEN WITH PEACH AND TARRAGON SAUCE

Flavours of the summer enhance the chicken to make this an ideal meal to enjoy outdoors. Accompany it with a chilled green (stick or snap) bean salad and new potatoes.

☐ Make a nick in the stalk end of each peach and plunge them into a bowl of boiling water for about 40 seconds. Lift out with a slotted spoon and slip off the skins.

☐ Halve the peaches and discard the stones (pits). Chop the peach flesh roughly, and put in a pan with the wine, lemon peel, chopped tarragon and salt and pepper, to taste.

☐ Simmer gently for 10 minutes; cool slightly, then liquidize until smooth.

☐ Poach (or steam) the chicken breasts gently in the chicken stock until tender. Remove the skin and allow to cool.

☐ Mix the cooled peach purée with the fromage frais. If the sauce is too thick, add a little liquid from poaching the chicken. Adjust seasoning.

☐ Arrange the chicken breasts on a serving dish, spoon the peach sauce over the top and chill for an hour. To serve, garnish with slices of peach and sprigs of fresh tarragon.

CORONATION CHICKEN (BELOW LEFT)

This dish was developed by the Cordon Bleu Cookery School in London to celebrate the Queen's Coronation in 1953. It remains a firm favourite, particularly for buffets. Serve with a simple rice salad.

☐ Heat the oil, add the onion and cook for 3 to 4 minutes. Stir in the curry powder and cook for a further minute.

☐ Add the purée (paste), wine, water, bayleaf and lemon slices. Simmer, uncovered, for about 10 minutes or until well reduced. Strain and cool completely.

☐ Gradually beat the cooled sauce into the mayonnaise, then add the apricot jam (preserve) and fromage frais or yogurt. Adjust the seasoning.

☐ Lightly coat the chicken pieces with the mayonnaise. Pile onto a serving dish and garnish with a light dusting of paprika and thin slices of cucumber.

Coronation Chicken

Tomato Salad with Chicken Liver Dressing

TOMATO SALAD WITH CHICKEN LIVER DRESSING

A more unusual way of using chicken livers, but nonetheless delicious. Vary the salad by adding thickly sliced mushrooms or sliced onions. The dressing is also good served with plain cooked chicken.

☐ First prepare the tomatoes. Make an incision in the stem end of each, and plunge in boiling water for 40 seconds. Drain and slip off the skins. Slice thinly onto the serving plate, and sprinkle with the chopped spring onions (scallions). Chill.

☐ To make the dressing, heat 30 ml/2 tablespoonfuls of the oil. Sauté the livers with the chopped garlic until they just begin to brown.

☐ Spoon the livers and garlic into a food processor or liquidizer and blend together with the mustard, eggs and vinegar. Gradually drizzle in the remaining oil.

☐ Stir in the coarsely crushed peppercorns and season to taste. Spoon over the chilled tomatoes and serve immediately, garnished with a spring onion (scallion) curl and some snipped chives. Accompany with brown bread.

SERVES 4

125 g/4 oz fresh spinach
4 boneless chicken breasts, skinned
(approx. 175 g/6 oz each)
50 g/2 oz smoked salmon slivers (or trimmings)
½ lemon, finely grated rind
salt and freshly ground black pepper
45 ml/3 tbsp sunflower oil
⅓ cup/90 ml/6 tbsp low calorie mayonnaise
15 ml/1 tbsp fresh dill, chopped
sprigs of dill

CHICKEN, SMOKED SALMON AND SPINACH ROULADE

These attractive 'pinwheels', accompanied by a dill mayonnaise and a crisp salad, are ideal for a summer lunch or picnic.

☐ Remove the thick stem part from each spinach leaf. Blanch spinach in boiling water for 1 minute, refresh in cold water and drain on absorbent paper (paper towel).

☐ Place each chicken breast between 2 sheets dampened greaseproof paper and flatten to approximately 1 cm/½ in thick, with a rolling pin. (Try to keep as neat a shape as possible.)

☐ Lay the drained spinach leaves over each chicken breast, smooth side down, then lay the smoked salmon on top and sprinkle over the grated lemon rind. Season to taste.

☐ Roll up, swiss roll (jelly roll) fashion, and secure with wooden cocktail sticks.

☐ Heat the oil in a shallow pan; add the chicken roulades and cook gently for 20 minutes, turning them occasionally until the chicken is tender.

☐ Allow to cool, then remove the cocktail sticks and wrap the cooked roulades in cling film (plastic wrap). Chill until required.

☐ To serve, slice the roulades and accompany with the mayonnaise, to which has been added the chopped dill, seasoned to taste. Garnish with dill sprigs.

CHICKEN CHANTILLY

This is an ideal fork or buffet dish. It is very decorative and can be made in advance and assembled prior to serving.

☐ Put half the oil, the lemon juice, wine, stock, mushrooms, onions, tomato and bayleaf into a pan. Season well, bring to the boil, then simmer, covered, for 6 to 10 minutes.

☐ Heat the remaining oil in a pan and stir-fry the rice until it begins to go opaque.

☐ Strain off the liquor from the mushroom and onion, reserving the vegetables, and add enough boiling water or stock (broth) to make the quantity up to 2 cups/500 ml/18 fl oz. Pour this onto the rice, cover and cook until all the liquid is absorbed and the rice is just tender, about 20 to 25 minutes. Remove bayleaf, stir in the mushroom and onion and leave to cool.

☐ Arrange the rice mixture in a circle on a flat dish, leaving a hollow in the centre.

☐ Take the chicken meat off the bone and coarsely chop. Fold in the mayonnaise and fromage frais. Season to taste with salt and pepper. Pile on top of the rice pilaff.

☐ Garnish the top of the chicken with crosswise strips of pimento (sweet red pepper). Place the lettuce leaves in the centre of the dish, and sprinkle with the sieved egg yolk. Mix the chopped egg white with the parsley and spoon a thin line around the edge of the rice. Serve chilled.

SERVES 4 TO 6

30 ml/2 tbsp vegetable oil
juice of ½ lemon
⅓ cup/90 ml/6 tbsp white wine
3–4 pickling onions (or shallots), sliced
1 cup/125 g/4 oz button mushrooms, wiped and sliced
⅔ cup/150 ml/¼ pt chicken stock (broth) plus extra, if needed
1 tomato, peeled and deseeded
1 bayleaf
1 ½ cups/175 g/6 oz long grain rice
1 × 1.5 kg/3 ½ lb chicken, cooked
1 ¼ cups/300 ml/½ pt low calorie mayonnaise
⅔ cup/150 ml/¼ pt fromage frais
salt and freshly ground black pepper

GARNISH

1 hard boiled (hard cooked) egg (yolk sieved, egg white chopped)
1 lettuce heart
strips of canned pimento (sweet red pepper)
30 ml/2 tbsp fresh parsley, chopped

Mediterranean Chicken Salad

MEDITERRANEAN CHICKEN SALAD

Fresh herbs make all the difference in this summer salad. For a change, substitute the ham with flaked tuna fish, and the basil with fresh tarragon.

☐ Cut the chicken and ham into neat strips. Cut the beans into 2.5 cm/1 in lengths and the potatoes into small chunks. Place in a large bowl.

☐ Halve or slice the tomatoes, depending on size. Cut the cucumber in half lengthways, scoop out and discard the seeds, then cut the flesh into matchsticks. Add to the bowl.

☐ Fold these ingredients together carefully, together with the freshly chopped herbs and olives.

☐ In a screw top jar, shake together the olive oil, wine vinegar, lemon juice, mustard powder, cayenne, sugar and seasonings until well blended. Pour over the chicken salad.

☐ Spoon the salad into a glass serving dish. Garnish the top with fresh anchovies, and sprigs of fresh herbs. Chill for at least one hour before serving to allow the flavours to develop.

SERVES 6

175 g/6 oz cooked chicken
125 g/4 oz cooked ham
175 g/6 oz French beans or green (string or snap) beans, lightly cooked
175 g/6 oz new potatoes, cooked
4 plum or cherry tomatoes (yellow or red variety)
½ cucumber, peeled
12 black olives
15 ml/1 tbsp each freshly chopped basil, parsley and chives
¼ cup/60 ml/4 tbsp olive oil
15 ml/1 tbsp white wine vinegar
15 ml/1 tbsp lemon juice
pinch dry mustard powder
pinch cayenne
pinch caster (fine) sugar
salt and freshly ground black pepper
6 anchovies
fresh herb sprigs to garnish

8 large flat mushrooms
15 ml/1 tbsp sunflower oil plus a little extra
1 small onion, finely chopped
1 clove garlic, finely chopped
25 g/4 oz boneless chicken (thigh or breast)
2 rashers lean smoked bacon, derinded
2 cups/125 g/4 oz fresh white breadcrumbs
15 ml/1 tbsp Worcestershire sauce
good pinch mustard powder
salt and freshly ground black pepper
1 egg, beaten
40 g/1 ½ oz Parmesan cheese, freshly grated
30 ml/2 tbsp milk
freshly chopped parsley to garnish

Oven temperature: 200 °C/400 °F/Gas 6

Country Mushrooms

250 g/8 oz shortcrust pastry
1 small onion, finely chopped
15 ml/1 tbsp sunflower oil
250 g/8 oz cooked chicken, finely chopped
1 firm avocado pear, peeled, stoned (pitted) and cubed
75 g/3 oz low fat cream cheese, cut into small knobs
15 ml/1 tbsp each freshly chopped tarragon, parsley and chives
3 eggs
scant cup/200 ml/7 fl oz milk
salt and freshly ground black pepper

GARNISH
thin slivers of peeled avocado dipped in lemon juice
chopped parsley or chives

Oven temperature: 190 °C/375 °F/Gas 5

COUNTRY MUSHROOMS

Large open field mushrooms are full of flavour on their own, but are also good topped with this savoury stuffing for a starter or light meal. Chicken livers could be used instead of chicken.

- ☐ Remove the stalks from the mushrooms and chop finely.
- ☐ Heat the oil in a pan, and sauté the onions and garlic until softened. Add the chopped mushroom stalks and cook for a further minute.
- ☐ Finely dice the chicken and bacon and add to the pan. Stir-fry for a further 2 minutes. Remove from the heat and mix in the breadcrumbs, Worcestershire sauce, mustard and seasonings. Stir in the beaten egg.
- ☐ Spoon the mixture into the mushroom caps to form neat mounds.
- ☐ Drizzle a small amount of oil over the top of each filled mushroom and then sprinkle with a little Parmesan cheese.
- ☐ Place the mushrooms on a large, lightly oiled baking tray (cookie sheet). Add the milk to prevent the mushrooms from drying out.
- ☐ Bake for 20 minutes. Serve hot, sprinkled liberally with chopped parsley.

Chicken and Avocado Quiche

CHICKEN AND AVOCADO QUICHE

Try the subtle combination of chicken, avocado and cream cheese. Courgettes (zucchini) sliced and blanched make a good alternative to avocado if you prefer.

- ☐ Roll out the pastry fairly thinly and use to line a 23 cm/9 in diameter loose-bottomed fluted flan ring. Place on a baking sheet (cookie sheet). Fill with a circle of greaseproof paper and baking beans. Bake 'blind' for 10 to 15 minutes.
- ☐ Cook the onion gently in the oil for 3 to 4 minutes. Scatter over the base of the pastry case. Add the chicken, avocado, cream cheese and herbs.
- ☐ Beat together the eggs, milk and seasoning, to taste. Pour into the pastry case. Cook for 35 minutes or until the filling is set.
- ☐ Serve either warm or cold, garnished with slices of avocado and freshly chopped herbs.

BAKED STUFFED SWEET (BELL) PEPPERS

When buying the sweet (bell) peppers, choose squat round peppers which still stand upright. Choose green, red, yellow or orange peppers, or even a mixture.

- ☐ Cut the tops off the peppers and remove the cores and seeds. Put the peppers in a basin, cover with boiling water and allow to stand for 5 minutes. Drain thoroughly and set aside.
- ☐ Heat half the oil in a large pan and sauté the onion until softened. Stir in the rice and mushrooms and cook for a further minute; add the stock (broth), bring to the boil and simmer, covered, for 15 minutes, until the rice is just tender and the stock absorbed.
- ☐ Stir in the tomato purée (paste) and the freshly chopped basil. Season to taste.
- ☐ Heat the remaining oil and sauté the chicken livers until lightly browned. Stir into the rice with the pinenuts.
- ☐ Spoon the rice mixture into the peppers and sprinkle them with the cheese.
- ☐ Arrange the peppers in an ovenproof dish. Pour a little water into the dish (just enough to cover its base) and cook for 35 minutes or until the peppers are tender. Serve hot, garnished with fresh basil leaves.

SERVES 4

4 even-sized sweet (bell) peppers
30 ml/2 tbsp sunflower oil
1 small onion, finely chopped
1 cup/125 g/4 oz long grain rice
¼ cup/50 g/2 oz button mushrooms, chopped
2 cups/450 ml/¾ pt chicken stock (broth)
¼ cup/60 ml/4 tbsp tomato purée (paste)
30 ml/2 tbsp fresh basil, chopped
salt and freshly ground black pepper
4–6 chicken livers, chopped
30 ml/2 tbsp pinenuts, toasted
30 ml/2 tbsp finely grated Parmesan cheese
fresh basil leaves to garnish

Oven temperature: 180 °C/350 °F/Gas 4

1 × 1 ½ kg/3 ½ lb roasting chicken with giblets
⅓ cup/90 ml/6 tbsp sunflower oil
250 g/8 oz squid, cleaned and chopped
2 large onions, chopped
2 large cloves garlic, chopped
250 g/8 oz tomatoes, skinned, seeded and chopped
1 bayleaf
1 sprig fresh thyme
200 g/7 oz live mussels, scrubbed and debearded
200 g/7 oz chorizo or other spicy sausage, cut
into chunks
500 g/1 lb Valencia or best risotto rice
175 g/6 oz shelled prawns (shrimp)
250 g/8 oz monkfish, cubed
1 sweet green (bell) pepper and
1 sweet red (bell) pepper, seeded and cut into
1 cm/1 in pieces
175 g/6 oz small French or green (string or snap)
beans, top and tailed
75 g/3 oz frozen peas (or 250 g/8 oz peas in pod)
50 g/2 oz mange tout, top and tailed
15 saffron strands, soaked in 30 ml/2 tbsp hot water
10 ml/2 tsp paprika
salt

GARNISH
2 lemons
freshly chopped parsley
8 unshelled prawns (shrimp)

PAELLA VALENCIANA

'Paella' is a traditional Spanish speciality, shared at celebrations and among friends. There are many local variations, but the essential ingredients are rice and saffron, with a choice of chicken, shellfish and vegetables. The word 'paella' refers to the huge round 'shallow pan or 'paelleras' this dish is cooked in, and because these pans could measure anything from 30 cm (12 in) to a metre (3 ft) across, they are usually placed on an open fire for cooking.

☐ Joint the chicken, and then carefully chop into 5 cm/2 inch squares, keeping the meat on the bones.

☐ Place the carcass, together with the giblets and 3 cups/170 ml/1 ¼ pints water, in a pan. Add any fish skin and bones and the herbs together with a little salt and pepper.

☐ In a large pan, heat 30 ml/2 tablespoonfuls of the oil and brown the chicken all over, for about 10 minutes. Add the squid, cover and simmer for 10 minutes.

☐ Add the onion and garlic and cook until soft and just turning golden.

☐ Add the tomatoes. Simmer the mixture, uncovered, until the tomatoes have reduced to a pulp. This will take about 10 minutes.

☐ Add the mussels and chorizo or sausage. Cover and cook for 2 to 3 minutes or until the mussels have opened. Remove the pan from the heat.

☐ Heat the remaining oil in a paella pan or large frying pan (skillet). When the oil is hot, add the rice and cook, stirring, for 3 to 4 minutes.

☐ Add the chicken mixture to the rice, together with the prawns, monkfish, peppers, beans, peas and mange tout, saffron (plus soaking liquid), paprika and salt. Cook, stirring, for 2 minutes.

☐ Pour on 2 ¼ cups/500 ml/18 fl oz of the strained stock. Bring to the boil, then reduce the heat immediately to a gentle simmer.

☐ Cook for 15 to 20 minutes, shaking the pan from time to time (do not stir), and adding a little more stock if the mixture is drying out.

☐ Five minutes before the end, add the unshelled prawns (shrimp).

☐ Garnish the paella with lemon wedges and freshly chopped parsley, and serve from the pan, accompanied with some good Spanish wine.

CHICKEN, MUSHROOM AND SPINACH LASAGNE

A tasty lasagne, accompanied with a crisp salad and crusty brown bread makes for easy and informal entertaining. Prepare the lasagne in advance and chill until you are ready to cook it.

☐ To make the chicken sauce, heat the oil in a pan and cook the onion gently until softened. Add the diced chicken and stir-fry until the chicken is firm and cooked through.

☐ In another saucepan, melt the butter. Add the flour and cook, stirring, for one minute. Remove from the heat and slowly blend in the milk, beating to a smooth sauce between each addition. Return to the heat and bring to the boil and cook for one minute. Season with the nutmeg, salt and pepper.

☐ Put a third of the sauce into a bowl and reserve. Add the chicken and onion mixture to the remaining sauce. Place a layer of damp grease-proof paper on the surface of both sauces to prevent a skin forming.

☐ For the mushroom and spinach mixture, heat the oil and cook the onion and garlic gently until softened. Add the mushrooms and cook gently for 10 minutes or until any liquid has evaporated.

☐ Cook the spinach briefly in a large covered saucepan until it has wilted (see Glossary, page 93) and reduced in volume. No need to add any water. Drain, squeeze out any excess liquid and then chop finely. Add to the mushroom mixture and season to taste.

☐ Lightly oil a deep rectangular ovenproof dish approx. 30 × 18 cm (12 × 7 in). Line the bottom and sides of the dish with some of the pasta and then layer with half the chicken sauce, pasta, spinach and mush-room sauce, more pasta, the remaining chicken sauce, pasta and the plain sauce.

☐ Sprinkle with the grated Parmesan and cook for 45 to 50 minutes or until bubbling and golden brown on top.

SERVES 6

CHICKEN & NUTMEG SAUCE

15 ml/1 tbsp sunflower oil
1 small onion, finely chopped
500 g/1 lb uncooked chicken meat, cut into 1 cm (½ in) cubes
½ cup/125 g/4 oz butter
scant cup/125 g/4 oz plain (all purpose) flour
3¾ cups/900 ml/1 ½ pt semi-skimmed milk
2.5 ml/½ tsp freshly grated nutmeg
salt and freshly ground black pepper

MUSHROOM & SPINACH MIXTURE

15 ml/1 tbsp sunflower oil
1 onion, finely chopped
3 cloves garlic, crushed (minced)
375 g/12 oz flat mushrooms, finely chopped
375 g/12 oz fresh spinach, washed
salt and freshly ground black pepper

300–375 g/10–12 oz green pre-cooked lasagne (approximately 12 sheets)
50 g/2 oz Parmesan cheese, freshly grated

Oven temperature: 190 °C/375 °F/Gas 5

CORIANDER (CILANTRO) CHICKEN WITH PILAU RICE

SERVES 4

15 ml/1 tbsp sunflower oil
8 chicken thighs
1 large onion, sliced
5 ml/1 tsp paprika
5 ml/1 tsp ground cumin
5 ml/1 tsp turmeric
2.5 ml/½ tsp dried thyme
freshly ground black pepper
1¼ cups/300 ml/½ pt well flavoured chicken stock
(broth) (see page 11)
25 g/1 oz pitted black olives
30 ml/2 tbsp fresh coriander (cilantro), finely chopped
squeeze lemon juice

PILAU RICE

30 ml/2 tbsp vegetable oil
¼ cup/50 g/2 oz whole blanched almonds, toasted
1 small onion, finely diced
¼ cup/50 g/2 oz sultanas or raisins
3 cups/375 g/12 oz long grain rice
3¼ cups/750 ml/1¼ pt boiling water
2.5 ml/½ tsp salt

Fresh coriander (cilantro) has a unique, pungent flavour.

☐ Heat the oil in a large pan and fry the chicken until an even, rich brown. Transfer to a plate.
☐ Add the onion to the remaining oil and cook until softened and golden. Stir in the paprika, cumin and turmeric and cook for a further minute. Add the thyme, black pepper and stock and bring to the boil.
☐ Return the chicken to the pan, skin side down. Cover and simmer for 1 to 1¼ hours or until the chicken is tender.
☐ Remove the chicken with a slotted spoon to a heated serving dish and keep warm.
☐ Reduce the sauce by rapidly boiling until it thickens. Stir in the olives, coriander (cilantro) and lemon juice. Season to taste and pour over the chicken.
☐ For the rice, heat the oil in a large pan and cook the onion until softened but not coloured. Add the toasted almonds, sultanas and rice, and cook for a further minute, stirring thoroughly.
☐ Add the boiling water and salt. Bring to the boil, then cover and reduce the heat to a simmer. Cook for 15 minutes, or until all the water has been absorbed and the rice is tender, but still firm. Fork the rice lightly and serve with the chicken.

SPEEDY CHICKEN LIVERS WITH PASTA

S E R V E S   4

250 g/8 oz dried pasta shapes
30 ml/2 tbsp vegetable oil
250 g/8 oz chicken livers, cleaned and sliced
50 g/2 oz lean bacon, derinded and chopped
2 small courgettes (zucchini), sliced
4 spring onions (scallions), trimmed and sliced
1 cup/125 g/4 oz button mushrooms, sliced
1 small sweet red (bell) pepper, halved and cut
into strips
30 ml/2 tbsp redcurrant jelly
⅔ cup/150 ml/¼ pt dry white wine or chicken
stock (broth)
10 ml/2 tsp freshly chopped sage
¼ cup/60 ml/4 tbsp natural yogurt or fromage frais
salt and freshly ground black pepper
freshly chopped parsley to garnish

This chicken liver dish makes an all-in-one lunch or supper dish. If you do not wish to use pasta, serve the chicken livers on a bed of boiled brown rice.

☐ Cook the pasta in boiling salted water until 'al dente'.
☐ Meanwhile heat the oil in a pan and add the chicken livers and bacon and stir-fry for 1 minute. Add the courgettes (zucchini), spring onion (scallions), mushrooms and peppers and cook for a further 2 minutes.
☐ Stir in the redcurrant jelly, wine or stock, sage and salt and pepper. Cover and simmer for 4 to 5 minutes.
☐ Drain the pasta. Fold the chicken livers together with the yogurt or fromage frais.
☐ Sprinkle thickly with chopped parsley and serve immediately.

Coriander (Cilantro) Chicken with Pilau Rice

S E R V E S   2   O R   4

1 clove garlic, chopped
2.5 cm/1 in piece fresh ginger, peeled and chopped
75 ml/5 tbsp soy sauce
¼ cup/60 ml/4 tbsp mirin (sweet rice wine) or
dry sherry
¼ cup/60 ml/4 tbsp sake
30 ml/2 tbsp sugar
500 g/1 lb boned and skinned chicken meat, cut into
2.5 cm/1 in cubes
6–8 spring onions (scallions), trimmed and cut into
2.5 cm/1 in lengths
175 g/6 oz mushrooms, halved
½ cucumber, sliced, to garnish

YAKITORI CHICKEN SKEWERS

Mirin is available from Japanese food shops – but if you cannot obtain it, substitute with a dry sherry. Serve these skewers either as a starter, or with plain boiled rice as a main course. Chicken livers are sometimes included in Yakitori.

☐ In a bowl mix together the garlic, ginger, soy sauce, rice wine, sake and sugar. Stir in the chicken cubes. Cover with cling film and leave to marinate for 1 to 2 hours.

☐ Thread the chicken onto bamboo skewers 15–20 cm/6–8 in long, alternating with the spring onions and mushrooms. Brush with the marinade and arrange under a preheated grill.

☐ Cook for 8 to 10 minutes, basting frequently with the marinade, and turning the skewers several times, until the chicken is cooked through.

☐ Serve immediately, garnished with cucumber slices.

N O T E

Soak bamboo skewers for 30 minutes before using to prevent them from burning.

CHICKEN SATAY

This delicious Malaysian speciality can be made well in advance and chilled until required. Also try a combination of chicken, pork and beef. Serve the satays either as part of an oriental meal, or as a meal on its own, accompanied with plain boiled rice.

☐ Cut the chicken into 1.25 cm/½ in cubes.

☐ Combine the marinade ingredients in a bowl. Add the chicken cubes and stir until well coated. Cover and refrigerate for 2 hours, preferably overnight.

☐ Thread the meat onto 8 small bamboo skewers (see *Note*). Grill (broil) or barbecue for 6 to 8 minutes, turning frequently. (Use metal skewers if cooking over charcoal.)

☐ Meanwhile, make the sauce. Heat the oil in a pan, add the onon and garlic and cook until softened. Gradually blend in the spices, honey, soy sauce and lemon juice. Stir well, then add the peanut butter and cook gently for 1 minute.

☐ Remove from the heat and blend in the creamed coconut and hot water. Return to the heat and gradually bring to the boil stirring continuously. Reduce heat and simmer for 5 minutes. Taste and add salt if required.

☐ Arrange the skewered chicken on a platter, garnish with lemon twists and spring onion curls. Serve the peanut sauce separately in a bowl.

NOTE

Soak bamboo skewers for 30 minutes before using to prevent them from burning.

SERVES 4

500 g/1 lb chicken breasts or thighs, boned and skinned

MARINADE
1 small onion, peeled and grated
45 ml/3 tbsp soy sauce
45 ml/3 tbsp sherry
30 ml/2 tbsp vegetable oil
30 ml/2 tbsp clear honey
1 clove garlic, chopped
10 ml/2 tsp tomato purée (paste)
2.5 ml/½ tsp hot chilli (chili) powder

SATAY SAUCE
15 ml/1 tbsp vegetable oil
15 ml/1 tbsp grated onion
1 clove garlic, minced
2.5 ml/½ tsp hot chilli powder
2.5 ml/½ tsp ground coriander
10 ml/2 tsp honey
10 ml/2 tsp soy sauce
10 ml/2 tsp lemon juice
6 tbsp/75 g/3 oz smooth peanut butter
15 g/½ oz creamed coconut
1¼ cups/300 ml/½ pt water
salt

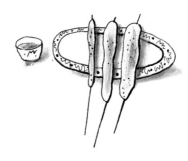

SESAME CHICKEN

While sesame seeds have a very subtle flavour and add a crunchiness here in contrast to the tender chicken strips, sesame oil is much stronger so the little used in this recipe is to add flavour rather than for frying purposes. Serve this dish hot with some stir-fried vegetables. It is also delicious cold, as a salad.

☐ Cut the chicken into fine diagonal shreds.

☐ Heat 15 ml/1 tbsp of the oil in a wok or frying pan (skillet) and stir-fry the chicken and dried chilli (chili) for 1 minute. Drain and transfer to absorbent kitchen paper.

☐ Wipe the wok clean, heat the remaining groundnut oil and add the sesame seeds. Stir-fry for 1 minute or until golden brown.

☐ Add the celery and stir-fry for a few seconds, before adding the remaining ingredients. Bring to the boil, return the chicken shreds and stir-fry for a further minute. Serve immediately.

SERVES 4

3 chicken breasts, boneless and skinned (approx. 175 g/6 oz each)
30 ml/2 tbsp groundnut oil
5 ml/1 tsp dried chilli (chili) granules (or flakes)
15 ml/1 tbsp sesame seeds
2 sticks celery, trimmed and thinly sliced
15 ml/1 tbsp soy sauce
15 ml/1 tbsp dry sherry
5 ml/1 tsp cider vinegar
2.5 ml/½ tsp salt
5 ml/1 tsp sesame oil

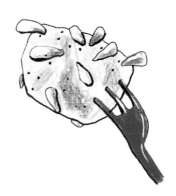

4 chicken breasts, skinned and part-boned
(approx. 175 g/6 oz each)
5 cm/2 in root ginger, peeled and cut into tiny
matchsticks
.2 medium onions, peeled and sliced
10 ml/2 tsp ground ginger
¼ cup/60 ml/4 tbsp light soy sauce
¼ cup/60 ml/4 tbsp dry sherry
30 ml/2 tbsp clear honey
salt and freshly ground black pepper
3 spring onions (scallions), trimmed and finely
chopped, to garnish

GINGERED CHICKEN WITH HONEY

This dish is very simply prepared and best accompanied with pilau rice (see page 54).

☐ Heat the oil in a pan and sauté the chicken pieces until golden.

☐ Add the fresh ginger and onions to the oil and sauté until the onions soften. Stir in the ground ginger and cook for a further 2 minutes.

☐ Return the chicken to the pan and cook for a minute more, then pour on the soy sauce, dry sherry and honey.

☐ Cover with a tight-fitting lid and simmer for 30 minutes or until the chicken is tender.

☐ Transfer the chicken and onions to a warm serving dish. Turn up the heat and boil the sauce to reduce it slightly. Season to taste.

☐ Spoon the sauce over the chicken and garnish with a sprinkling of spring onions (scallions). Serve hot.

Gingered Chicken with Honey

CHICKEN WITH BLACK BEANS

500 g/1 lb chicken pieces (thighs, wings, breasts)
15 ml/1 tbsp soy sauce
15 ml/1 tbsp dry sherry or rice wine
5 ml/1 tsp sugar
10 ml/2 tsp cornflour (cornstarch)
30 ml/2 tbsp groundnut oil
15 ml/1 tbsp finely chopped fresh ginger
4 cloves garlic, finely chopped
30 ml/2 tbsp black beans, rinsed and coarsely
chopped
2 spring onions (scallions), finely chopped
½ sweet red (bell) pepper, cut into
2.5 cm/1 in squares
⅔ cup/150 ml/¼ pt chicken stock (broth)

Black soya beans are available from good Chinese supermarkets, and are sold either canned or packed in plastic bags (they need rinsing before use). These fermented, slightly salted beans partner the garlic and fresh ginger perfectly – to give a distinctive flavour, reminiscent of Chinese home cooking.

☐ Chop the chicken pieces into 5 cm/2 in chunks. Mix the soy sauce, dry sherry, sugar and cornflour (cornstarch). Stir into the chicken pieces and leave to marinate for 1 hour.

☐ Drain the chicken, discarding any marinade. Heat half the oil in a wok. Add the ginger and stir-fry briefly, then add the garlic and black beans. Cook for 2 to 3 minutes.

☐ Add the chicken pieces and stir-fry for 4 to 5 minutes until they are browned. Add the spring onion (scallion), red (bell) pepper and stock (broth), reduce heat and simmer for 10 minutes.

☐ Serve immediately with plain boiled rice.

TROPICAL STIR-FRY

The wonderful thing about stir-fry recipes is that any number or combination of ingredients can be used. Serve with plain boiled rice.

☐ Stir-fry the onion in half the oil for 3 minutes. Add the remaining oil, garlic and the chicken and stir-fry briskly until the chicken is evenly coloured and almost tender.

☐ Add the sunflower seeds and cashew nuts and stir-fry for a further minute. Add the mango, kiwi, kumquats and salt and pepper to taste. Stir fry for a further 2 to 3 minutes.

☐ Sprinkle with flaked coconut and serve immediately.

SERVES 4

1 small onion, finely chopped
¼ cup/4 tbsp sunflower oil
1 clove garlic, crushed (minced)
2 boneless chicken breasts (approx. 175 g/6 oz each), skinned and cut into thin strips
15 ml/1 tbsp sunflower seeds
40 g/1 ½ oz salted cashew nuts
½ ripe, pink skinned mango, stoned and thinly sliced
2 kiwi fruit, peeled and sliced
4 kumquats, halved
salt and freshly ground black pepper
30 ml/2 tbsp flaked coconut

Tropical Stir-Fry   *Turmeric Chicken*

TURMERIC CHICKEN

Very spicy, and full of Eastern promise – cardamom, dates, almonds and the characteristic yellow turmeric. Accompany with plain boiled rice and a refreshing cucumber or tomato salad to calm down the palate!

☐ Heat the oil in a pan, and sauté the chicken legs until golden brown. Remove to one side.

☐ Add the onion to the pan and sauté until golden brown. Reduce the heat and stir in the spices. Cook for 1 minute.

☐ Return the chicken legs to the pan. Sprinkle in the flour and gradually blend in the stock. Bring to the boil, then simmer for 30 minutes, or until the chicken is tender.

☐ Mix in the almonds, dates, yogurt and half the fresh coriander (cilantro). Simmer gently for a further 10 minutes.

☐ Serve hot, garnished with the remaining coriander (cilantro).

SERVES 6

¼ cup/60 ml/4 tbsp vegetable oil
6 chicken leg portions (approx. 200 g/7 oz each)
2 medium onions, chopped
15 ml/1 tbsp ground coriander
5 ml/1 tsp turmeric
5 ml/1 tsp ground cumin
2.5 ml/½ tsp ground cardamom
2 pinches hot chilli (chili) powder
30 ml/2 tbsp plain (all purpose) flour
3 cups/750 ml/1 ¼ pt chicken stock (broth)
¼ cup/50 g/2 oz blanched almonds, coarsely chopped
¼ cup/50 g/2 oz dates, stoned and coarsely chopped
⅔ cup/150 ml/¼ pt natural low fat yogurt or fromage frais
30 ml/2 tbsp fresh coriander (cilantro) chopped
salt

1 × 1.5 kg/3½ lb oven-ready chicken
30 ml/2 tbsp vegetable oil
2 medium onions, peeled and thinly sliced
10 ml/2 tsp paprika
½ cup/125 ml/4 fl oz dry white wine
500 g/1 lb tomatoes, deseeded and chopped
(or 1 × 425 g/14 oz can tomatoes)
15 ml/1 tbsp tomato purée (paste)
2 whole canned pimentos (sweet red pepper),
roughly chopped
bouquet garni
salt
¼ cup/60 ml/4 tbsp natural yogurt
15 ml/1 tbsp chopped parsley

PAPRIKA CHICKEN

Paprika chicken uses, as the name implies, the subtle, milder dried red pepper – never to be confused or substituted for hotter members of the family like Cayenne or chilli (chili). Serve this warming dish with noodles or pasta shells.

☐ Joint the chicken into 8 pieces (*see page 10*), and remove the skin where possible.

☐ Heat the oil in a large pan and sauté the chicken until browned. Remove and set aside. Add the onions to the pan and cook until softened.

☐ Sprinkle in the paprika and cook for a further minute. Blend in the wine.

☐ Return the chicken pieces to the pan together with the tomatoes, purée (paste), pimentos (sweet red peppers), bouquet garni and salt to taste. Cover and simmer for 45 minutes.

☐ Transfer the chicken to a serving dish to keep warm. Rub the contents of the pan through a sieve. Return to rinsed pan and reheat. Season to taste.

☐ Swirl in the yogurt and pour over the chicken pieces. Sprinkle with the chopped parsley. Serve immediately.

PARMESAN BAKED CHICKEN

A topping rich with tomatoes, herbs and Italian cheeses embraces succulent breasts of chicken. Serve with plain new potatoes and fresh spinach.

☐ Heat half the oil in a pan and sauté the onions, garlic and celery until softened. Stir in the tomatoes, purée (paste), Tobasco, herbs and sugar. Season with salt and pepper. Simmer, uncovered, for 25 to 30 minutes.

☐ Sprinkle the skinned chicken breasts with lemon juice. Dip each breast into the egg and then the seasoned flour. Shake off any excess.

☐ Heat the remaining oil in a non-stick frying pan and sauté the chicken breasts for 5 minutes, turning halfway through, until golden brown. Drain on absorbent kitchen paper.

☐ Lay the chicken in an ovenproof dish and cover with half the Mozzarella cheese. Pour over sauce, top with the remaining cheese, and sprinkle with Parmesan.

☐ Bake for 25 to 30 minutes or until bubbling and golden.

☐ Serve, garnished with fresh watercress.

SERVES 4

4 boneless chicken breasts (approx. 150 g/5 oz each)
30 ml/2 tbsp olive oil
2 medium onions, finely chopped
2 cloves garlic, finely chopped
1 stick celery, chopped
1 × 425 g/14 oz can chopped tomatoes
15 ml/1 tbsp tomato purée (paste)
few drops Tobasco
5 ml/1 tsp fresh basil, chopped
5 ml/1 tsp fresh marjoram, chopped
5 ml/1 tsp sugar
30 ml/2 tbsp lemon juice
1 egg, beaten
25 g/1 oz plain (all purpose) flour, seasoned
150 g/6 oz Mozzarella cheese, grated
30 ml/2 tbsp grated Parmesan cheese
salt and freshly ground black pepper
fresh watercress, to garnish

Oven temperature: 180 °C/350 °F/Gas 5

Chicken Thighs in Pernod

Parmesan Baked Chicken

CHICKEN THIGHS IN PERNOD

A quick and easy standby, good enough on its own with crusty brown bread, or served with fresh vegetables.

☐ Heat the oil in a large pan. Cook the chicken for 8 minutes, browning all sides. Reduce the heat, add the shallots or onion and water. Cover the pan and simmer gently for 30 to 35 minutes or until the chicken is tender.

☐ Remove the lid, increase the heat and pour in the Pernod. Set alight with a match, and turn off the heat. When the flames die down, scrape up any sediment from the bottom of the pan.

☐ Remove the chicken portions to a warm serving dish. Season the remaining juices with salt and pepper and bring to the boil. Spoon over the chicken and serve, garnished with a sprinkling of parsley.

SERVES 4

8–12 chicken thighs (depending on size)
30 ml/2 tbsp vegetable oil
2 shallots or 1 small sweet onion, finely chopped
¼ cup/60 ml/4 tbsp water
⅓ cup/90 ml/ 6 tbsp Pernod
salt and freshly ground black pepper
chopped fresh parsley, to garnish

SERVES 4

500 g/1 lb chicken livers
1 tbsp/15 g/½ oz butter
15 ml/1 tbsp vegetable oil
1 large onion, diced
1 clove garlic, crushed
2.5 ml/½ tsp hot chilli (chili) powder
3 tomatoes, peeled, deseeded and sliced
⅔ cup/75 g/3 oz button mushrooms, sliced
30 ml/2 tbsp tomato purée (paste)
½ cup/125 ml/4 fl oz red wine or Marsala
2.5 ml/½ tsp thyme, freshly chopped
pinch ground bayleaves
5 ml/1 tsp Worcestershire sauce
salt and freshly ground black pepper
⅔ cup/150 ml/¼ pt fromage frais
freshly chopped parsley, to garnish

BLUSHING CHICKEN LIVERS

Here the chicken livers are quickly cooked in a spicy tomato sauce. They are good served with jacket potatoes, creamed potatoes or noodles and a green salad.

☐ Rinse the chicken livers and pat dry on kitchen paper towel.

☐ Heat the butter and oil in a saucepan. Sauté the onions and garlic until lightly browned and softened.

☐ Sprinkle in the chilli (chili) powder and stir in the chicken livers. Cook for 4 minutes.

☐ Add the tomatoes and mushrooms and cook for a further minute. Then stir in the tomato purée (paste), red wine or Marsala, herbs and Worcestershire sauce. Simmer, uncovered, for 4 minutes. The liquid will reduce a little.

☐ Season to taste and stir in the fromage frais.

☐ Serve immediately, garnished liberally with chopped parsley.

FRAGRANT CHICKEN PARCELS

These parcels, containing fresh herbs, yogurt and succulent chicken, can be cooked in the oven, over a steamer or even in with the barbecue charcoals. Whichever method is chosen, the result is deliciously aromatic. Accompany with new potatoes and green (string or snap) beans.

☐ In a shallow dish, blend together the first nine ingredients. Make a couple of slashes in the chicken breasts, then coat the chicken with the sauce. Leave in the dish, cover and marinate for 2 to 3 hours in a cool place.
☐ Place each breast in the centre of a large piece of foil. Spoon over any remaining marinade. Wrap the foil up around the chicken, sealing well.
☐ Cook for 20 to 25 minutes or until the chicken is tender. Serve in the foil parcels, opened and garnished with lemon slices and fresh chervil.

NOTE
If you would prefer to steam the chicken parcels they will take 25 to 30 minutes.

SERVES 4
5 ml/1 tsp cornflour (cornstarch)
grated rind ½ lemon
45 ml/3 tbsp natural yogurt
3 cardamom pods, seeds only, crushed
2.5 ml/½ tsp coriander seeds, crushed (cilantro)
15 ml/1 tbsp freshly chopped chervil
10 ml/2 tsp freshly chopped tarragon
10 ml/2 tsp Dijon mustard
salt and freshly ground black pepper
4 boneless chicken breasts (approx. 175 g/6 oz) skinned

GARNISH
lemon slices
fresh chervil

Oven temperature: 190 °C/375 °C/Gas 6

Chicken Jurassiene

Fragrant Chicken Parcels

CHICKEN JURASSIENNE

Although this recipe uses whole chicken breasts, you can, if you prefer, cut the chicken into 'goujons' (wide strips) before crumbing them. Serve accompanied with mixed salad.

☐ Slightly flatten the chicken breasts between 2 sheets of dampened greaseproof paper.
☐ Mix together the flour, nutmeg and salt and pepper and thoroughly coat the chicken breasts.
☐ Dip the floured chicken breasts in the beaten egg, then into a mixture of breadcrumbs and cheese, pressing the crumbs well against the chicken flesh.
☐ Place on a lightly oiled baking tray (cookie sheet). Drizzle the oil over the breasts. Cook for 30 minutes or until golden brown and crisp.
☐ Serve hot, garnished with lemon slices.

SERVES 4
4 chicken boneless breasts (approx. 150 g/5 oz each) skinned
½ cup/50 g/2 oz plain (all purpose) flour
2 pinches grated nutmeg
salt and freshly ground black pepper
2 eggs, lightly beaten
1½ cups/75 g/3 oz fresh breadcrumbs
40 g/1½ oz Gruyère cheese, finely grated
¼ cup/60 ml/4 tbsp sunflower oil
1 lemon, sliced, to garnish

Oven temperature: 200 °C/400 °F/Gas 6

FRUITY CHICKEN KEBABS WITH CURRIED HONEY GLAZE

Kebabs are perfect for both a summer barbecue or a winter supper. They can be made well in advance and the ingredients can be varied to suit your own preference. Fruit and a curried honey marinade are delicious with chicken and help to keep it moist during cooking.

□ Shake all the marinade ingredients together in a screw top jar.
□ Cut the chicken into neat 2.5 cm/1 in cubes. Place in a bowl and pour over the marinade. Cover and keep in a refrigerator for 6 hours, or until required.
□ Stretch the bacon rashers with the back of a knife. Cut each into half and form into rolls.
□ Alternately thread pieces of chicken, apricot halves, banana chunks and bacon rolls onto skewers.
□ Brush with the remaining marinade and cook for 10 to 15 minutes under a pre-heated grill (broiler) turning and basting frequently, until the chicken is cooked and sizzling.
□ Serve warm with crusty bread and salad.

NOTE

If you are using bamboo skewers, soak these in water for 30 minutes beforehand to prevent them from burning.

SERVES 4
MARINADE
⅓ cup/90 ml/6 tbsp clear honey
¼ cup/60 ml/4 tbsp light olive oil
rind and juice 1 orange
2 cloves garlic, crushed
15 ml/1 tbsp Worcestershire sauce
5 ml/1 tsp coriander seeds, crushed
5 ml/1 tsp curry powder
salt

4 large boneless chicken breasts, skinned
8 rashers streaky bacon, diced
16 dried apricot halves (non-soak variety)
2 firm bananas, cut into 2.5 cm/1 in slices
15 ml/1 tbsp lemon juice

BARBECUED ROAST CHICKEN

This recipe makes a change from the traditional roast. The chicken is coated with a barbecue sauce and roasted in the delicious juices. Alternatively, the sauce can be poured over an equivalent quantity of chicken drumsticks and thighs and cooked for 1 hour instead. Serve with jacket potatoes or boiled rice and seasonal or stir-fried vegetables.

□ Place the chicken in a roasting tin (pan). Rub the oil over the chicken and season with salt and pepper.
□ Roast the chicken for 30 minutes.
□ In a screw-top jar or bowl, mix together the remaining ingredients, apart from the garnish. Remove the chicken from the oven and pour the sauce over the bird.
□ Roast for a further 1 hour, basting frequently with the sauce. The skin will turn a rich, dark-brown colour.
□ Serve the chicken hot, garnished with fresh sprigs of watercress.

SERVES 4
1 x 1.5 kg/3½ lb oven-ready chicken
15 ml/1 tbsp olive oil
salt and freshly ground black pepper
1 medium onion, finely diced
¼ cup/60 ml/4 tbsp cider or sherry vinegar
¼ cup/2 tbsp tomato purée (paste)
15 ml/1 tbsp clear honey
5 ml/1 tsp mustard powder
1 clove garlic, crushed
fresh watercress, to garnish

Oven temperature: 200 °C/400 °F/Gas 6

Fruity Chicken Kebabs with Curried Honey Glaze

8 to 12 chicken drumsticks
30 ml/2 tbsp vegetable oil
1 small onion, chopped
1 carrot, cut into small julienne strips
(see Glossary, page 93)
1 sweet green (bell) pepper, seeded and diced
1 small can pineapple slices in natural juice
(approx. 200 g/7 oz)
30 ml/2 tbsp clear honey
10 ml/2 tsp Worcestershire sauce
30 ml/2 tbsp tomato ketchup
15 ml/1 tbsp mango chutney
30 ml/2 tbsp red wine vinegar
15 ml/1 tbsp cornflour (cornstarch)
2.5 ml/½ level teaspoon salt

Oven temperature: 200 °C/400 °F/Gas 6

SWEET AND SOUR CHICKEN DRUMSTICKS

Sweet and sour dishes have long remained a firm favourite. Although any joint of chicken can be used, the dark meat has always proved most popular. Serve the dish with plain boiled rice.

☐ Heat the oil in a pan and sauté the chicken drumsticks until browned. Remove to one side.

☐ Add the onion and cook until softened. Stir in carrots and cook for a further 3 minutes. Stir in the sweet green (bell) pepper.

☐ Strain the pineapple juice into a measuring jug, and make up to 1¼ cups/300 ml/½ pt with cold water. Chop the pineapple roughly and add to the pan together with the juice.

☐ Stir in the honey, Worcestershire sauce, tomato ketchup and chutney.

☐ Blend together the vinegar and cornflour (cornstarch). Add to the pan with the salt. Bring to the boil stirring, cook for 1 minute.

☐ Pour the sauce into a shallow (approx. 5 cups/2 pt) ovenproof dish. Arrange the drumsticks on top. Cover and cook for 20 minutes.

☐ Remove the cover and cook for a further 15 minutes.

☐ Serve the drumsticks with a little sauce. Pass the remaining sauce separately.

SKEWERED CHICKEN

A healthy and nutritious way of serving chicken to children. Delicious hot with rice or jacket potatoes, or cold as part of a packed lunch.

☐ Skin and cut the chicken breasts into small, even-sized cubes (approx. 2 cm/¾ in). Thread them onto 8 small wooden kebab skewers, which have been soaked for ½ hour to stop them burning.

☐ Mix together the peanut butter, yogurt, orange rind and black pepper to taste. Spoon the mixture evenly over the skewered chicken. Cover loosely and chill for 4 hours.

☐ Arrange the skewers on the rack of the grill (broiler) pan, and spoon over any remaining marinade. Grill (broil) for 4 minutes under a moderate heat. Turn the skewers and grill (broil) for a further 3 minutes.

☐ Mix the orange juice with the honey and spoon over the kebabs. Return to the grill (broiler) for a further 2 minutes.

☐ Serve hot or cold, garnished with orange segments and watercress.

SERVES 4

3 boneless chicken breasts (approx. 175 g/6 oz each)
30 ml/2 tbsp smooth peanut butter
30 ml/2 tbsp low fat natural yogurt
freshly ground black pepper
grated rind ½ orange
juice 1 orange
15 ml/1 tbsp clear honey

GARNISH
peeled orange segments
sprigs of watercress

39

30 ml/2 tbsp olive oil
8 shallots or pickling onions, peeled
seasoned flour
4 part-boned chicken breasts
(approx. 200 g/7 oz each)
1 ¼ cup/300 ml/½ pt chicken stock (broth)
15 ml/1 tbsp Dijon mustard
5 ml/1 tsp fresh thyme
2 cups/250 g/8 oz tiny button mushrooms, wiped
salt and freshly ground black pepper
fresh thyme sprigs to garnish

4 chicken legs or breasts (approx. 175 g/6 oz each)
8 sprigs thyme
4 rashers lean bacon, derinded
15 ml/1 tbsp vegetable oil
1 large onion, chopped
2 cloves garlic, finely chopped
8 tomatoes, skinned, deseeded and shredded
5 ml/1 tsp tomato purée (paste)
5 ml/1 tsp plain (all purpose) flour
1 ¼ cups/300 ml/½ pt dry white wine
salt and freshly ground black pepper

GARNISH
8 × 1 cm/½ in slices French bread, toasted
30 ml/2 tbsp parsley, freshly chopped

DIJON CHICKEN WITH MUSHROOMS

Very quick to prepare for the unexpected guest. Although Dijon mustard is used in this recipe, try experimenting with wholegrain or one of the speciality mustards.

☐ Heat the oil in a saucepan, add the shallots or onions and sauté until golden brown.

☐ Skin the chicken breasts and dust lightly with the seasoned flour. Add to the pan and sauté until golden brown all over.

☐ Add the chicken stock (broth), mustard, thyme and salt and pepper to taste. Cover and simmer for 15 minutes.

☐ Add the mushrooms and continue simmering, uncovered, for a further 15 minutes.

☐ Serve immediately, garnished with sprigs of fresh thyme.

CHICKEN PROVENCAL

Tomatoes, thyme and garlic provide a taste of Provence. Omit the bacon rashers, if you wish – but you may need to add extra oil. Add the thyme sprigs directly to the pan. Delicious with plain potatoes and green (string or snap) beans.

☐ Skin the chicken joints. Lay a sprig of thyme on the top and underside of each joint and wrap a piece of bacon around it, securing with a cocktail stick.

☐ Heat the oil in a pan and sauté the chicken until the joints and bacon are a deep golden colour. Remove and put to one side.

☐ Add the onion and garlic to the pan and cook until softened. Stir in the tomatoes and purée (paste) and cook for a further minute.

☐ Sprinkle the flour over the onion mixture and stir well until blended. Gradually pour in the wine. Bring to the boil, stirring, until slightly thickened. Reduce heat. Season to taste.

☐ Return the chicken joints to the pan, cover, and simmer for 45 minutes or until the chicken is tender.

☐ Transfer the chicken to a warm serving dish (remove the cocktail sticks). Bring the sauce to the boil and let it bubble until it is reduced to the consistency of single (light) cream.

☐ Pour the sauce over the chicken. Garnish with freshly toasted French bread and a generous sprinkling of the chopped parsley.

Dijon Chicken with Mushrooms

4 medium sized potatoes
2 large carrots, peeled and chopped
3 sticks celery, chopped
175 g/6 oz shredded green cabbage
4 chicken legs (approx. 175 g/6 oz each)
¼ cup/25 g/1 oz seasoned flour
30 ml/2 tbsp vegetable oil
15 ml/1 tbsp fresh thyme, chopped
salt and freshly ground black pepper
1 ¼ cups/300 ml/½ pt beef stock (broth)
⅔ cup/150 ml/¼ pt Guinness or stout
15 ml/1 tbsp dark soft brown sugar
1 egg, beaten
chopped fresh thyme, to garnish

Oven temperature: 180 °C/350 °F/Gas 4

COUNTRY CHICKEN HOTPOT

Reminiscent of the Irish hot pot, made even more authentic by the addition of some Irish stout!

- ☐ Peel the potatoes; cut two of the potatoes into thin slices, and chop the other two.
- ☐ Mix the chopped potato with the carrot, celery and cabbage.
- ☐ Dust the chicken legs with seasoned flour. Heat the oil in a large pan and sauté the chicken legs until lightly golden on all sides. Add the thyme, and salt and pepper to taste.
- ☐ Place half of the mixed vegetables in the base of a deep casserole. Top with the chicken legs and then the remaining vegetables.
- ☐ Mix the stock (broth), Guinness or stout and brown sugar together and pour over the contents of the casserole.
- ☐ Overlap the potato slices in concentric circles on top of the vegetables and chicken. Brush with a little oil.
- ☐ Cover with a piece of lightly oiled foil and cook for 1 hour.
- ☐ Remove the foil. Brush the potato crust with the beaten egg. Return to the oven for a further 35 to 40 minutes. Serve sprinkled with chopped thyme.

ROAST CHICKEN WITH WALNUT AND PEAR STUFFING

Pears are often neglected in savoury cooking, but here they prove their worth in a delicious nutty stuffing.

☐ Mix the chopped pear with the breadcrumbs, walnuts, ginger and salt and pepper to taste. Mix in the egg yolk to bind the stuffing together.

☐ Push the cloves into the skin of the half lemon and place inside the chicken.

☐ Press the pear stuffing into the neck cavity of the chicken and fold the remaining neck skin neatly underneath the bird, to secure the stuffing.

☐ Place the chicken in a roasting dish, season with salt and pepper, and brush all over with honey. Cook in a preheated oven for 1¼–1½ hours. Baste several times during cooking, spooning the honeyed juices over the chicken.

☐ To prepare the glazed pears for the garnish, gently heat together the pear slices and the honey in the pan, turning the pears from time to time until they become translucent.

☐ To serve, carve or joint the bird and serve accompanied with some stuffing and a few glazed pear slices.

SERVES 6

1 small ripe pear, peeled, cored and chopped
1 cup/50 g/2 oz fresh wholemeal breadcrumbs
25 g/1 oz chopped walnuts
generous pinch ground ginger
salt and freshly ground black pepper
1 egg yolk
5 cloves
½ lemon
1 × 1.5 kg/3½ lb oven-ready chicken
30 ml/2 tbsp clear honey
GARNISH

1 pear, cored and sliced
15 ml/1 tbsp clear honey

Oven temperature: 200 °C/400 °F/Gas 6

SPICED SPATCHOCK

Although spatchcock refers generally to a roasting chicken, poussins (Cornish game hens) are just as good and more convenient to prepare and serve. If they are barbecued, baste them with any remaining marinade and a little olive oil. Serve with a salad and potatoes boulangère.

☐ Split the birds in half by cutting down one side of the backbone. Open the birds out and turn them over.

☐ Rub the poussins (Cornish game gens) with the lemon juice and olive oil. Place in a shallow heatproof dish.

☐ In a bowl, mix together the lemon rind, shallot, garlic, peppercorns, coriander, juniper berries and allspice. Press the mixture over the birds.

☐ Tuck small pieces of rosemary in around the wing and leg joints.

☐ Cover and leave to stand for 2 hours or refrigerate for 8 hours or overnight.

☐ Sprinkle the poussins (Cornish game hens) with a little Tabasco and cook under a hot grill (broiler) for 20 to 30 minutes, turning and basting occasionally with the juices.

☐ Serve, with any remaining pan juices, garnished with sprigs of fresh rosemary.

SERVES 2

2 poussins (Cornish game hens),
approx. 500 g/1 lb each
grated rind and juice 1 small lemon
15 ml/1 tbsp olive oil
1 shallot or small sweet onion, finely chopped
1 clove garlic, finely chopped
10 ml/2 tsp green peppercorns, crushed
5 ml/1 tsp coriander (cilantro) seeds, crushed
4 juniper berries, crushed
2.5 ml/½ tsp ground allspice
2 sprigs rosemary, plus extra for garnish
dash Tabasco

4 part-boned chicken breasts
(approx. 200 g/7 oz each),
50 g/2 oz celery
50 g/2 oz carrots, peeled
50 g/2 oz green (string or snap) beans, top and tailed
⅔ cup/150 ml/¼ pt chicken stock (broth)
1 bayleaf
30 ml/2 tbsp white wine
1 bunch watercress, trimmed of coarse stalks
2 spring onions (scallions), trimmed and chopped
75 g/3 oz fromage frais
5 ml/1 tsp cornflour (cornstarch) blended with
5 ml/1 tsp water
salt and freshly ground black pepper

CHICKEN BREAST WITH WATERCRESS SAUCE

This chicken dish looks very fresh and colourful and provides sufficient vegetables to need only the addition of new potatoes when serving. If you have a steamer, cook the chicken over the stock for 25 to 30 minutes. The vegetables can also be steamed briefly.

☐ Skin the chicken breasts and season lightly.

☐ Prepare the vegetables and cut into julienne strips (*see Glossary, page 93*).

☐ In a pan, bring the stock to a steady simmer. Add the chicken and bayleaf and cover with a tight fitting lid.

☐ Cook gently for 35 to 40 minutes or until the chicken is tender.

☐ Transfer the chicken to a warm serving plate. Add the seasoning and the spring onions to the stock. (Remove and discard the bayleaf.) Bring to the boil and rapidly bubble until the stock has reduced a little.

☐ Add the white wine and the watercress, reserving a few leaves for the garnish. Remove the heat and allow to stand for one minute for the watercress to wilt.

☐ Meanwhile, cook the vegetable julienne in boiling water until just 'al dente' – no more than 5 minutes. Drain and keep warm.

☐ Strain the stock into a measuring jug. Transfer the watercress and spring onions (scallions) to a food processor or blender and add ⅓ cup/90 ml/6 tbsp stock, the fromage frais and the blended cornflour (cornstarch). Purée to a smooth sauce. Season to taste.

☐ Reheat gently, stirring, until thickened. Adjust the consistency of the sauce with a little more stock if desired.

☐ To serve, place each chicken breast on a plate. Spoon over the vegetables julienne and pour the watercress sauce around the chicken. Garnish with the reserved watercress leaves.

CHICKEN IN SWEET RED (BELL) PEPPER AND ALMOND SAUCE

A colourful chicken dish, enhanced with a nutty, spicy flavour that requires little accompaniment other than plain boiled rice to help mop up the juices.

☐ Skin the chicken breasts and cut into pieces approximately 4 cm × 1 cm (2 in × ½ in). Heat a third of the oil in a pan and cook the chicken for 5 minutes. Drain and transfer to a plate.

☐ Combine the onion, ginger, garlic, almonds, sweet red (bell) peppers, cumin, coriander, turmeric, cayenne and salt in a food processor or liquidizer. Blend to a smooth paste.

☐ Heat the remaining oil. Add the paste and cook for 10 to 12 minutes, stirring occasionally. Add the chicken pieces, water, star anise, lemon juice and black pepper to taste. Cover, reduce the heat and simmer gently for 25 minutes or until the chicken is tender. Stir once or twice during cooking.

SERVES 4

4 boneless chicken breasts, (approx. 175/6 oz each)
⅓ cup/90 ml/6 tbsp sunflower oil
I medium onion, roughly chopped
2 cm/I in fresh ginger, peeled
3 cloves garlic
25 g/I oz blanched almonds
375 g/12 oz sweet red (bell) pepper, deseeded and chopped
15 ml/I tbsp ground cumin
10 ml/2 tsp ground coriander (cilantro)
5 ml/I tsp turmeric
pinch Cayenne pepper
2.5 ml/½ tsp salt
⅔ cup/150 ml/¼ pt water
3 whole star anise (a Chinese spice)
30 ml/2 tbsp lemon juice
freshly ground black pepper

Chicken in Sweet Red (Bell) Pepper and Almond Sauce

CHICKEN À LA KING

This dish can be made a day or two in advance and kept covered in the refrigerator until required. Serve with plain boiled rice, to help mop up the juices.

☐ Skin the chicken breasts and cut into bite-size pieces.

☐ Heat the butter and half the oil in a large frying pan. Add the mushrooms and sweet (bell) peppers and stir-fry until the peppers are just turning tender. Transfer, with a slotted spoon, onto absorbent kitchen paper (paper towel), to drain.

☐ Add the remaining oil to the pan and add the chicken pieces in a single layer. Sauté until golden brown. Season with salt and pepper.

☐ Stir in the stock, fromage frais and the brandy and cornflour (cornstarch), blended together. Continue to stir, over a low heat, until the sauce begins to thicken. Gently simmer, uncovered, for 5 minutes. Check seasoning and adjust if necessary.

☐ Stir in the mushrooms and sweet (bell) peppers and cook for a further 3 to 4 minutes. Serve on a bed of rice, garnished with fresh watercress.

SERVES 6

6 boneless chicken breasts (approx. 150 g/5 oz each)
2 tbsp/25 g/I oz butter
30 ml/2 tbsp vegetable oil
300 g/10 oz button mushrooms, thickly sliced
I sweet red (bell) pepper, deseeded and cut into 2.5 cm/I in squares
I sweet yellow (bell) pepper, deseeded and cut into 2.5 cm/I in squares
I sweet green (bell) pepper, deseeded and cut into 2.5 cm/I in squares
few strands saffron, soaked in 30 ml/2 tbsp boiling water
⅔ cup/150 ml/¼ pt chicken stock (broth)
I ¼ cups/300 ml/½ pt fromage frais or low fat yogurt
30 ml/2 tbsp brandy or medium sherry
10 ml/2 tsp cornflour (cornstarch)
salt and freshly ground black pepper
fresh watercress, to garnish

1 × 1.25/1.75 kg (3½–4 lb) roasting chicken
30 ml/2 tbsp vegetable oil
4 lean bacon rashers, derinded and chopped
12 baby onions or shallots, peeled
2 cloves garlic, chopped
5 cups/1.2 l/2 pt French red table wine
15 ml/1 tsp brandy
15 ml/1 tbsp tomato purée (paste)
2 sprigs fresh thyme
2 bayleaves
2 sprigs fresh parsley
300 g/10 oz small dark-gilled mushrooms
salt and freshly ground black pepper
15 ml/1 tbsp plain (all purpose) flour
15 ml/1 tbsp butter, softened
30 ml/2 tbsp freshly chopped parsley

COQ AU VIN

Originally the French farmer's simple stew using farmhouse chickens and wine from a neighbouring vineyard, this dish is now a classic. As with many casseroles and stews, the flavour will improve if made a day or two in advance.

☐ Joint the chicken into 8 portions (see page 10).

☐ Heat the oil in a large, heavy-based pan. Add the chicken in one single layer and sauté until evenly browned all over. Remove from the pan. Drain off all but 15 ml/1 tbsp fat from the pan.

☐ Add the bacon, baby onions or shallots and garlic to the pan and fry until the onions are golden. Stir in the red wine, brandy, tomato purée (paste), fresh herbs and seasoning, to taste.

☐ Return the chicken to the pan. Bring to the boil, then reduce the heat, cover and simmer for 40 minutes. Stir in the mushrooms and simmer, uncovered, for a further 10 minutes. Adjust seasoning, if necessary.

☐ Transfer the chicken, onions and mushrooms to a warm serving plate. Discard the herbs. Bring the sauce to a steady boil and drop in tea-spoonfuls of the creamed flour and butter. (This is called beurre manie.) Whisk continuously, until all the mixture has been added. Simmer for 10 minutes to cook the flour and thicken the sauce.

☐ Pour the sauce over the chicken, then sprinkle with the freshly chopped parsley. Serve immediately, accompanied with fresh vegetables.

CHICKEN AND RICOTTA WITH FRESH TOMATO AND BASIL SAUCE

A very pretty dish, fresh with the vibrant colours of the tomato sauce and spinach filling. Accompany with a salad and new potatoes.

☐ Flatten each chicken breast, in turn, by beating between 2 pieces of damp greaseproof paper with a rolling pin.

☐ Remove the spinach leaves from the main stalk and wash well. Shake well, put in a large dry pan and cook until wilted and reduced in volume. Drain, squeezing well to remove excess liquid. Chop finely.

☐ Mix together the spinach, ricotta, pinenuts and seasoning. Divide the filling between the breasts and spread over each, leaving 1 cm (½ in) gap on one long edge. Roll up each 'roulade' starting with the opposite edge, and secure loosely with strong cotton or fine string. Wrap each breast in a piece of foil and lay in an ovenproof dish.

☐ Pour in the stock (broth) and poach gently for 30 minutes, or until the chicken is cooked through.

☐ Meanwhile make the sauce. Chop the tomatoes roughly. Heat the oil and cook gently until softened. Add the tomatoes, purée (paste), sugar and seasoning. Simmer for 30 minutes.

☐ Liquidize until smooth. Check the seasoning, then stir in the chopped basil. Keep warm until required, then divide between 6 warm plates.

☐ To serve, remove the chicken, each breast cut into neat slices and arrange on top of the sauce on each plate. Garnish with fresh basil leaves.

SERVES 6

6 boneless chicken breasts, skinned
(approx. 175 g/6 oz each)
500 g/1 lb fresh spinach
175 g/6 oz ricotta cheese
¼ cup/50 g/2 oz pinenuts
salt and freshly ground black pepper
1¼ cups/300 ml/½ pt chicken stock (broth)

SAUCE

500 g/1 lb fresh tomatoes, skinned
15 ml/1 tbsp sunflower oil
1 small onion, diced
15 ml/1 tbsp tomato purée (paste)
5 ml/1 tsp caster (fine) sugar
salt and freshly ground black pepper
30 ml/2 tbsp chopped fresh basil

GARNISH

fresh basil leaves

Oven temperature: 200 °C/400 °F/Gas 6

*4 boneless chicken breasts
(approx. 175 g/6 oz each),*

MARINADE
*⅔ cup/150 ml/¼ pt white wine
¼ cup/60 ml/4 tbsp Pernod
juice of 1 large lemon
15 ml/1 tbsp olive oil
5 ml/1 tsp crushed black peppercorns
pinch dill weed
pinch sea salt*

STUFFING
*½ cup/125 g/4 oz low fat cream cheese
12 peeled prawns (shrimp), chopped
5 ml/1 tsp chopped parsley
2.5 ml/½ tsp fennel seeds
salt and freshly ground black pepper*

GARNISH
sprigs fresh fennel or dill

Oven temperature: 190 °C/375 °F/Gas 5

WOODS' MARINATED CHICKEN WITH PRAWN (SHRIMP) AND FENNEL

Long marinating is the secret to the success of this recipe. It is essential to allow the chicken flavours to fully develop. Start preparing this dish a day in advance.

☐ Lay the chicken breasts in a shallow dish. Pour over the marinade ingredients. Cover and chill for 24 hours.

☐ Remove chicken breasts and reserve the marinade.

☐ Beat together the stuffing ingredients. Make a deep incision in the side of each chicken breast, and spoon the stuffing mixture into the pocket. Secure the edges with a cocktail stick. Transfer to a shallow roasting dish.

☐ Cook for 25 minutes or until the chicken is tender. Carefully remove and discard the chicken skin and cocktail sticks. Transfer the chicken to a warm serving plate.

☐ Deglaze the juices in the roasting dish with the reserved marinade. Place over a high heat and boil the marinade until it has reduced slightly. Check seasoning. Pour over the chicken.

☐ Garnish with sprigs of fresh dill or fennel, and accompany with fresh garden vegetables.